A Layman's Commentary

Volume 6

Acts
of the
Apostles

John Devine

BALBOA.
PRESS
A DIVISION OF HAY HOUSE

Balboa Press books may be ordered through booksellers or by contacting:

Balboa Press
A Division of Hay House
1663 Liberty Drive
Bloomington, IN 47403
www.balboapress.com.au
1-(877) 407-4847

ISBN: 978-1-4525-1371-3 (sc)
ISBN: 978-1-4525-1372-0 (e)

Printed in the United States of America

Balboa Press rev. date: 03/22/2014

Book of the Acts of the Apostles

This Book records the activities of the disciples from the final days of the ministry of Jesus on earth and the developments that led to the birth of the Church in Jerusalem. The Gospel quickly spread throughout Judea and into Samaria with the realization that the message of salvation that comes by faith in Jesus Christ alone was not just for the Jewish people but was available to people of all nations who would receive Jesus as Savior and Lord.

A major centre was established at Antioch in Syria. Mission endeavor then took the message into Asia Minor and Southern Europe, all the way to Rome, the centre of the then known world within the space of thirty years.

The coming and influence of the Holy Spirit is paramount to the growth of the early Church and continues to the present time. The Book may equally be called the Acts of the Holy Spirit.

From the sermons of Peter, Stephen and Paul and the actions of the other disciples the basic doctrine of the early Church is revealed. This basic unity confirms the inspiration of the Holy Spirit 2Tim 3:16.

CONTENTS

Acts of the Apostles

Introduction – After the resurrection Jesus spent a month explaining the purpose of his death, referring to the Old Testament Scriptures and in instructing the disciples for the task of establishing the church when he left them Lk 24:25-27. He told them to wait for the Holy Spirit and then he ascended into heaven 1:4,9. The Book of Acts records the events that followed from then until the church was firmly developed extending from the beginnings in Jerusalem to Judea and Samaria, then to Asia Minor, Greece and Rome. The story is still being written today in the lives of believers.

Author – Luke the physician and colleague of the apostle Paul who also wrote the Gospel of Luke wrote the Book of Acts. Being a professional Luke meticulously investigated the events of the life of Jesus and the impact of the resurrection on the disciples. Together the Gospel of Luke and the Acts of the Apostles provide a history of the beginning of the Christian Church. That these two Books written by one who was not an apostle were accepted by the early church bears testimony to the authenticity and high standard of the work both in accuracy and detail. Luke also includes many events and details which integrate with the letters of the apostles to enhance the understanding of the early history. These writings were not prepared as historical documents but as personal records and communications – they are selective and are in narrative form. Yet they are the only recorded history of the beginning and growth of the early church. It is by the providence of God that they have been prepared and preserved in the form we have them in today.

Acts was written in the early AD 60's around the time of Paul's first imprisonment in Rome. There is no record of his death around AD 67 or his intervening ministry. The Jewish rebellion in AD 67 and the fall of Jerusalem in AD 70 are not mentioned. As these events were predicted by Jesus and the destruction of the Temple meant the end of the Levitical priesthood it would have been most relevant to Luke Mt 24:2 had they been recent events.

Luke joined Paul at Troas (near Troy) in northwest Asia Minor around AD 50 on Paul's Second Mission Journey 16:10. He had contact with key people as sources – Philip 21:8, James and the elders 21:17,18 and Mark Phm 1:24. He continued to assist Paul both as physician and coworker until the end of Acts.

Period – The record begins shortly after the resurrection of Jesus and continues to the imprisonment of Paul (Saul) for the Gospel in the early AD 60's. This was a period of some 30 years.

Theme – The birth and growth of the early Church The coming of the Holy Spirit was pivotal in the formation of the church. Jesus explained that the disciples would need the power provided by the Holy Spirit coming upon them in order for them to be his witnesses 1:8. This occurred ten days later at Pentecost and was largely responsible for the sudden boldness and determination of the disciples and the exceptional growth of the new movement.

The Person and Work of the Holy Spirit The presence, influence and direction of the Holy Spirit in establishing the early church is recognized throughout the Book of Acts (ref p79). The same presence and power of the Holy Spirit is available and required by the disciples of Jesus and the church today (ref p83).

The teaching of Jesus about the work of the Holy Spirit is recorded in John's Gospel chapters 14 to 16 (ref p83). As Jesus is the head of the Church so the Holy Spirit may be seen as the executive director carrying out the will of Jesus through the lives of his obedient people.[1]

Reliability of the New Testament Documents - "The universal claims which the New Testament makes upon mankind are so absolute and the character and works of its chief Figure (Jesus) so unparalleled that we want to be as sure of its truth as we possibly can - in point of fact there is much more evidence for the New Testament than for any other ancient writing of comparable date" - Bruce, theologian and historian.[2]

Special Features - Luke was a Gentile from Antioch in Asia Minor, a doctor and well educated historian. He is mentioned three times in the Letters of Paul together with Mark so the two had considerable contact Col 4:14; 2Tim 4:11; Phm 1:24. The term 'we' mentioned in Acts indicates that Luke accompanied Paul on some of his mission journeys 16:10-17.

He accepted the testimony of the resurrection appearances of Jesus 1:3; the ascension 1:9 and the Pentecost experience including speaking in tongues 2:1-4 from eyewitnesses he had come to trust. He verified and embraced the miracles and reports of healing during the life of Jesus. This was confirmed by the evidence of his own personal experience in the travels with the apostle Paul. As such he has prepared a most credible record of the events of the early church.

Luke provides information about the conditions of the people and places where the events took place which would otherwise have not been known. He also reports the importance of women both in service and leadership as taught by Jesus 1:14; 2:1,4; 2:18.

Structure of the Book

Birth of the Church - the beginning of the church in Jerusalem after the ascension – the first days - 1:1 to 2:47

The Early Church – Establishing the Church in Jerusalem over the next three years - 3:1 to 7:60

The Church Scattered – In Judea and Samaria - 8:1 to 9:31

Acceptance of the Gentiles The spread of the church north to Antioch in Syria during the next decade - 9:32 to 11:18

The Church at Antioch - Preparing for major mission to the nations of the world - 11:19 to 12:25

To the Ends of the Earth - Growth of the church from Antioch into Asia Minor and Europe from around AD 45 to the early AD 60's -

*   **First Mission Journey** – Paul and Barnabas in Asia - 13:1 to 15:35
*   **Second Mission Journey** – Paul and Silas in Europe - 15:36 to 18:22
*   **Third Mission Journey** – Return to Asia and Europe - 18:23 to 21:16
*   **Journey to Rome** – Paul taken to Rome to wait trial - 21:17 to 28:31

BIRTH OF THE CHURCH AD 30 (1:1 to 2:47)

1:1,2 **Reason for Writing** The Book of Acts is the continuation of a narrative which begins prior to the birth of Jesus and concludes with the impact of his life throughout the Roman empire.

Luke clearly states his reason for writing the Book and connects it with the Gospel under his authorship.

He confirmed that there were already many written accounts of the events surrounding Jesus available at the time (around AD 60) Lk 1:1,2. He investigated the events of the resurrection and reappearance of Jesus to satisfy himself with the veracity of the claims to the extent that he became a follower of the risen Lord.

The Gospel is Luke's *former book* - he had investigated and documented these things before he compiled the Acts of the Apostles.

1:3 **The Resurrection** The life and death of Jesus are as well attested as any other historical person from the first Century. Virtually all modern scholars of antiquity agree that Jesus existed. Apart from church

theologians there are statements from over ten secular writers of the first and second centuries which refer to Jesus or the activities of his followers from as early as AD 66. They include Roman historians and authorities who dealt with the Christian believers in matters of daily affairs. These records put the historical fact of the life and death of Jesus beyond doubt.[3]
However it is the resurrection from the dead that is the crucial aspect of belief in Jesus as the Messiah - he *was declared with power to be the Son of God by his resurrection from the dead: Jesus Christ our Lord Rom 1:1-4.* It was the intervention of God to vindicate and authenticate the work of his Son.

The Empty Tomb One must consider the possible options for the events of his resurrection which include -
• Jesus did not die on the cross but survived and reappeared. Yet he was declared dead by a professional soldier who confirmed it by a death blow, otherwise his legs would have been broken as was the custom Mk 15:44,45; Jn 19:32-34. These things were all witnessed by John the disciple who remained at the crucifixion site till the end Jn 19:35-37
• His body was discarded as a common criminal and could not be found. Yet his body was obtained by official request from Pilate by Joseph and Nicodemus, two members of the Sanhedrin, placed in an identified new tomb of Joseph and prepared in accord with Jewish burial customs Jn 19:38-42. This fulfilled another prophecy concerning his death Is 53:9
• His body was taken from the tomb by the religious authorities in case of resurrection rumors. Had this been the case they could easily have produced the body later to quell the good news
• The declaration of Jesus that he would rise from the dead was not of concern to the Sanhedrin. Yet for fear of his resurrection they requested a guard be placed at the entrance of the tomb with an official seal on the stone Mt 27:62-66
• His body was stolen by the disciples. That this could have occurred is refuted by the placement of the guard. Yet this suggestion was widely circulated and cannot account for the change in the disciples moral Mt 28:11-15
• The greatest conformation of his resurrection is the transformation in the lives of the followers three days after his crucifixion. The disciples and women were crushed by disappointment and resignation – their hopes had been dashed and their leader had been executed Lk 24:19-24. They had come to believe that he was the Son of Man, the Messiah

Dan, 7:13 and that he would introduce the new kingdom delivering them from the domination of Rome – now he was gone. Yet this small band of demoralized supporters was changed within the day to challenge the Jewish and Roman authorities on pain of death and take the Good News to the world - **He has risen, just as he said!** Mt 28:6.

Further proof of the resurrection is in the fact that faith in Jesus not only took hold in the hostile world of the Roman Empire but that it became the dominant faith of the empire within 300 years and continues to impact the lives of many people today.

The motivation of the early believers was - **I have seen the Lord** Jn 20:18. **The missing body of Jesus** is a central issue of history and a fact that each person must address - for on it rests one's eternal future - *that Christ died for our sins according to the Scriptures, that he was buried, that he was raised on the third day according to the Scriptures 1Cor 15:3,4.* Luke examined the facts and concluded that *he showed himself to these men and gave convincing (infallible) proofs that he was alive v3.*

1:3 Speaking about the Kingdom of God After the surprise of the resurrection Jesus appeared to all the disciples many times over a period of forty days v3. There were five hundred present on one occasion most of whom were still living at the time of Paul's writing AD 56 - they would have been accessible as eye witnesses to Luke the historian for his investigation 1Cor 15:5-8.

During this period Jesus taught them, reinforcing all the truths he had told them during his ministry about the kingdom of God. He explained to them again how the Scriptures were fulfilled by his life, suffering, death and resurrection Lk 24:25-27,32,44-48. Now they could comprehend and appropriate his words. This would form the basis for the teaching of the believers. "The New Testament is in the Old Testament concealed; The Old Testament is in the New Testament revealed" - Missler, cryptologist and Bible expositor.[4]

Appearances There are twelve specific reported appearances of Jesus after the resurrection-

• Mary Magdalene who had received healing and who lingered at the tomb Mk 16:9; Jn 20:10-18
• The women who went to the tomb to prepare the body Mt 28:9
• Simon Peter who had denied Jesus Lk 24:34; 1Cor 15:5
• Two followers on the way to Emmaus Mk 16:12; Lk 24:13-35
• The ten disciples in the upper room Mk 16:14; Lk 24:36; Jn 20:19,20

Acts of the Apostles

- Thomas, who was not present with the ten and doubted Jn 20:24-29
- James, the brother of the Lord who became head of the Council in Jerusalem 1Cor 15:7
- The great catch of fish when the seven disciples were again commissioned Jn 21:1-7
- A gathering of five hundred at one time 1Cor 15:5-8
- On a mountain in Galilee when the disciples received the Great Commission Mt 28:16-20
- At the Ascension on the Mount of Olives with the eleven disciples Acts 1:6-12
- Paul received a vision in the form of a blinding light that changed his life Acts 9:3-9; 1Cor 15:8.

These dramatic appearances help to understand why the disciples came to embraced all the claims that Jesus had made – that he was the Messiah, the Son of God, One with the Father and the only way of salvation Mt 26:63,64; Jn 14:6. They also explain the commitment and dedication of the early believers.

1:4,5 **The importance of waiting** He gave them final instructions. He told them not to leave Jerusalem but to wait for the coming of the Holy Spirit, the gift promised by God the Father v4,5; Lk 3:16.

We recognize that God is working his purposes out Phil 2:12,13. We must learn to wait on him through prayer and reading the Word so that we can walk humbly under his leading in our daily lives Is 40:29-31.

1:6,7 **The desire to know** The disciples were interested in many matters expecting his imminent return. He told them there are things we are not to know v7. But one thing is important – the extension of the kingdom of God.

1:8 **You will be my witnesses** A witness is one who has seen or knows by personal experience - who can speak from personal involvement - who declares the truth. Those of us who have a relationship with Jesus through faith now have the privilege and joy of telling others about him and the good things the Lord has done for us. This was the most important command of Jesus to those who put their faith in him Mt 28:18-20.

This can be a daunting task at times. We cannot be effective in our own ability. However God has provided the Holy Spirit to give the ability and power to testify successfully. We are coworkers together with God 2Cor 6:1. **The Promise of Jesus -** *You will receive power when the Holy Spirit comes on you and you will be my witnesses v8;* Lk 3:16.

The purpose of the coming of the Holy Spirit is to empower the believer to witness to Jesus. He provides the leading and the words to say Jn 15:26,27. He also provides conviction of sin and the rebirth Jn 16:8-11. The role of the Holy Spirit was explained by Jesus in the upper room on the night before he was crucified (ref p83).

The influence of the Holy Spirit in the growth of the church is seen throughout the Book of Acts. He directs and empowers the believer today. We must recognize his presence and learn to respond to his leading in our daily lives as the early disciples did Gal 5:25. They were to be witnesses in Jerusalem, in all Judea, Samaria and to the ends of the earth. For today this means not just in your home town or with local people but wherever the Holy Spirit may lead you. This was the last instruction of Jesus.

1:9-11 **The Ascension** Jesus then ascended into heaven v9. The disciples saw him depart from them in a cloud of light as at the Transfiguration Mk 9:2,3. God is Spirit and the resurrected Person of Jesus was translated into the spiritual dimension of the heavenly realm Eph 1:20,21.

It is into this realm that we have been born again when we receive Jesus as Savior and Lord Jn 1:12,13; 3:5-8. There also we will be translated - imperishable, raised in glory and power, spiritual - to inherit eternity Eph 2:5-7; 1Cor 15:42-44. The disciples were told that he will return in the same way 1:11; Mt 24:30; Rev 19:16 - that we also may be where he is! Jn 14:1-4.

The first time Jesus came to save - the second time will be as judge Rev 1:7.

1:12-15 **Waiting for the Promise** They returned to the upper room in Jerusalem, where Jesus had instituted the New Covenant Lk 22:17-20. They were Peter and Andrew, James and John, Philip and Bartholomew (Nathanael?), Thomas and Matthew, James (the Zealot) and Thaddaeus (Judas?) and Simon the Zealot Mt 10:1-4; Mk 3:16-19; Lk 6:12-16.

There were some 120 believers - including women and Mary the mother of Jesus and the younger half-brothers, James and Jude, Joses and Simon Mt 15:55. They had all been transformed by the resurrection v13.

They waited patiently as instructed by Jesus, joining together in prayer 1:4.

1:15-20 **Individual Responsibility** With the joy of the resurrection we have the sad outcome of Judas Iscariot. He was one of the initial twelve disciples chosen by Jesus – *he was one of our number and shared in this ministry v17.* Judas spent three years under the ministry of Jesus Mk 3:13-19. He was a capable leader, given opportunity and responsibility for the finance and the provisions of the group. Yet he abused his position of trust Jn 12:5,6. Despite the special calling he betrayed his Lord by arranging a quiet location for the arrest Mk 14:10,11. It could not have been for the thirty pieces of silver, the price of a slave – which he soon regretted Mt 27:3-5. Perhaps he wanted to bring about revolt. Whatever the reason he took action against the Lord. Jesus confirmed that although his death was necessary the one who betrayed him must take responsibility for his action Mt 26:23,24. Judas had the opportunity to be witness to the resurrection of Jesus but his decision ended in despair and loss. Every day each of us are faced with choices and decisions and must be aware that we will be held accountable. May our choices be true to our values and contribute to the greater goals and objectives of our lives.

1:21-26 **The Apostles** Matthias was appointed to replace Judas as one of the twelve who would bear testimony to the life and resurrection of Jesus v26. They would become the leaders of the early believers - called apostles, one who is sent with authority - along with Paul, who became apostle to the Gentiles.

2:1-4 **Pentecost and the Coming of the Holy Spirit** This encounter occurred ten days later (fifty days after Passover when Jesus was crucified 1Pet 1:18,19). Pentecost marked the end of the grain harvest and celebrated the Harvest Festival, a time of thanksgiving and one of the three important Feasts for the Jews Ex 23:14-17. This was most significant -
• Jesus had been crucified as our Passover Lamb Lk 22:19,20; 1Cor 5:7,8
• He rose again from the dead three days later as our Firstfruits (of those who will rise again to eternal life) 1Cor 15:20-23
• Now Pentecost was corresponding with the harvest of mankind through the Holy Spirit 1:8.
The Feast of Pentecost drew people, Jews and Jewish converts, from around the known world.
On this Pentecost those in the upper room were all suddenly filled with the Holy Spirit just as Jesus had said 1:8. They spoke in tongues (an unlearned prayer language) and declared the wonders of God – giving praise to God. They began suddenly to boldly witness to Jesus v4; 1:8. They were clothed with power from on high.
Clothed with Power v4 - The 'power from on high' was promised by Jesus Lk 24:49 and provides the courage and ability to witness to him.

It is important for effective service to receive this baptism of the Holy Spirit and to seek fresh filling through consecration every day (ref p84). It requires that we be fully committed to the work of proclaiming the Gospel.

We need to learn to wait humbly on the Lord to know his presence and will and be ready to respond to his leading. It is our privilege to cooperate with God's Spirit in all areas of ministry and life.

"When Christians humble themselves and consecrate their all afresh to Christ and ask for this power, they will often receive such a baptism that they will be instrumental in converting more souls in one day than in all their lifetime before" - Finney, Evangelist.[5]

2:5-13 The People's Response There were many visitors in Jerusalem for the Pentecost Festival - people of fifteen nationalities from throughout the known world are listed. They were Jews and converts to Judaism who had come to celebrate the Feast. They were amazed and perplexed as they heard in this praise expressed by the believers the message of Jesus being told in their own native languages v5-12.

2:14-41 **Peter's First Sermon**

Peter took the lead - his Gospel message was –

- an explanation for this outpouring of the Holy Spirit v14
- he saw this outpouring as introducing the 'last days' v17
- he referred to the Scriptures of the Old Testament for the confirmation of the event v12-21
- the relevance of this prophetic event is that *everyone who calls on the name of the Lord will be saved v21,36*
- he emphasized the manhood of Jesus as our representative to take the penalty for our sin v22
- it was God's set purpose and foreknowledge for Jesus to be crucified, to remove the offense of sin v23
- God raised Jesus from the dead confirming acceptance v23,24
- this was supported by prophetic words of King David from Scripture v25-32; Ps 16:8-11 - David was declared to be a prophet, foreseeing the resurrection of Jesus one thousand years before it took place! v30
- those present were witnesses that God had raised Jesus to life – confirmation of the resurrection v32
- Jesus has been exalted to the right hand of God – confirmation of his deity v32

Acts of the Apostles

- as a result God poured out the Holy Spirit as promised v33,34 - this was foretold that God would pour out his Spirit on all people v17; Joel 2:28-32
- God has made Jesus both Lord and Christ (Hebrew – Messiah; Greek – Christ; English - the Anointed One) v36
- it is necessary to repent and be baptized in the name of Jesus Christ for the forgiveness of sin v38
- those who do will receive the gift of the Holy Spirit themselves v38; Is 44:3; Ezk 36:26,27
- the promise of the Holy Spirit is available to all who will receive it v39.

This message contains the core doctrine of the Christian faith (ref p67). The importance of the Person of Jesus and his crucifixion and resurrection as confirming the means of forgiveness of sin is central. It was also supported by quotations from the Scriptures showing that Jesus had fulfilled many of the Old Testament prophecies as he had taught them 1Pet 1:3-5. The Word of God (Scriptures) is the basis for knowledge and growth for the believer 20:32.

The doctrine expressed in this first of Peter's sermons is contained in his letters 1Pet 1:18-21. It is confirmed by Paul *that Christ died for our sins according to the Scriptures, that he was buried, that he was raised on the third day* 1Cor 15:3-8. It was the focus of the preaching and teaching of the early church and remains so today. This truth distinguishes the Christian faith from all other philosophies.

The unified content of the messages confirms the inspiration of the Holy Spirit 1Tim 3:16.

Death and Resurrection v23,24 – On a number of occasions Jesus predicted his death and that he would rise again on the third day Mt 12:40; 16:21; 20:18,19: 26:2; Mk 8:31; 9:31; 10:33,34; Lk 24:7; 24:46; Jn 2:19.

This prediction was extremely difficult for the disciples to understand – Peter even denied that it could happen Mt 16:21,22; Mk 9:32. They were looking for a new kingdom, not the death of their leader.

But Jesus had to die in order to remove the offense of sin from before God - *God made him who had no sin to be sin for us, so that in him we might become the righteousness of God 2Cor 5:21;* Jn 1:29; 6:40; 8:24; Heb 9:26-28; 10:14.

Jesus had to rise again in order to demonstrate that God had accepted his selfless sacrifice and that sin could be forgiven through faith in his name – *whoever believes in the Son has eternal life Jn 3:35,36;* Rom 1:2-4. This was all according to God's plan – his set purpose and foreknowledge v23; 4:28; Eph 1:9,10; 1Cor 2:7,8.

The object of his coming was to give his life a ransom for many Mt 20:28. After the resurrection the disciples remembered the words of Jesus and this truth became the focus and the motivation for their declaration Lk 24:7,8; 24:47. It is this truth that each person must address.

Power from on High The eloquence and content of Peter's address bear testimony to the forty days of Spirit-inspired teaching by Jesus and the indwelling presence of the Holy Spirit in the life of the disciples 1:1,2; 2:4; Lk 24:49. Recall that just fifty days earlier Peter had denied knowing Jesus and fled from the scene of the trial. He had earlier declared that Jesus should not suffer execution Mt 16:21,22. He was now empowered by the Holy Spirit! Jesus had declared **on this rock I will build my church** - that is, on the testimony of faith that Jesus is *the Christ, the Son of the living God Mt 16.18.*

The Triune God v33 A further truth was presented in Peter's sermon which he now appreciated - that the God who is One reveals himself as Father, Son and Holy Spirit. This is the main distinction between the one true God and the man-made gods of the world. This truth comes from revelation alone. The Scriptures explain that God is One and that he is revealed as three distinct Persons 2Cor 13:14. We primarily encounter the Trinity as –

• **Father** – the Creator who sustains all things by the Word of his power and determines the fate of the universe and all people v33; Rom 1:7; 6:4

• **Son** – the Savior who died for the sins of the world and rose again as Lord v33; 9:20; 13:33; Rom 1:3,4; 5:8. It was the declaration of Jesus to be the Son of God that really confirmed the understanding of the Trinity Jn 5:25,26; 10:30; 11:4.

• **Holy Spirit** – the indwelling presence of God in the heart of the believer to guide and empower in the work of ministry v33; Jn 14:26. Jesus also explained the Person of the Holy Spirit in the upper room (ref p83).

This understanding of the triune nature of God was foreshadowed in the Old Testament. It was expounded by Jesus during his ministry Jn 10:30; 14:16,17. Now, after the resurrection and experience of Pentecost, Peter could give full voice to this new revelation 2:33,36,38 - confirmed in his letters and in the letters of Paul 1Pet 1:2; 2Cor 13:14.

While it is a mystery to the human mind, known only by revelation, the relationship with the Father, the Son and the Holy Spirit is the experience of all those who put their trust in Jesus Jn 14:43.

2:36 **Jesus – both Lord and Christ** While the disciples accepted Jesus as their Lord during his ministry there was caution about recognizing him as the Messiah. When Peter confessed this based on what he had seen and heard he was told not to declare it until the right time Mt 16:16-20. In his first address Peter boldly gave full emphasis to the authority of Jesus as Lord and Christ (Messiah, the Anointed One). As a result of the resurrection and ascension they were convinced that Jesus had been exalted to the highest place by God and that the time was now right to make it known v32-36. This title, Jesus Christ the Lord, was identified with Jesus before birth and became the focus of the believer's ministry 11:17; 15:26; 28:31; Mt 1:21; Lk 2:10-12. In the last day *at the name of Jesus, every knee should bow, in heaven and on earth and under the earth, and every tongue confess that Jesus Christ is Lord, to the glory of God the Father Phil 2:10,11.* The awesome significance of this recognition and declaration relates to the fact that God is declared as Lord, king and judge Is 33:22; 43:15; 44:6; 45:23.

Lord of All Some see Jesus as a good moral teacher or another prophet – they give intellectual ascent. We are not given this option based on the claims Jesus made about himself Jn 5:18; 11:25,26; 14:6. The response of the first disciples showed they understood this – they did not respond to his teaching but to his resurrection. Jesus is either Lord of all or not at all 10:36; 1Cor 8:6.

2:41 **The Response** Many of the people came under conviction of sin v37. It is this awareness of wrongdoing and coming short of the standard of God that brings a person to realize the need of the Savior. About 3,000 people accepted Jesus as Savior that day and were baptized as an outward sign of inner repentance and following the example of Jesus v41.

All who are far off v39 The message was first preached to Jewish people, all Israel v22,36. At first the disciples did not comprehend that Jesus had died for all nations despite his teaching Mt 28:19; Jn 3:14-16. Even at the appointment of the deacons the believers consisted of Jews and Jewish converts 6:1. It was not until Philip's time in Samaria and Peter's encounter with Cornelius that the universal nature of God's plan of salvation was realized – *I now realize how true it is that God does not show favoritism but accepts men from every nation who fear him* *and do what is right* *10:34;* 8:14. This all happened under the direction of the Holy Spirit.

2:42-47 The First Community – Characteristics

How would the 3,000 new believers have been discipled?
- they studied and applied the teaching and the Word in their daily lives
- they met together for fellowship, for the 'breaking of bread' and for prayer
- they were all filled with awe as wonders occurred
- they had everything in common and gave to those in need
- they continued to meet together regularly, every day!
- they met in their homes 'breaking bread' and having common meals with glad hearts and praising God.

Five Essentials of Growth From this experience we can identify five invaluable aspects of the believer's life that will promote growth –
- **Prayer** – Jesus prayed as a natural part of his life. He modeled prayer for his disciples and for us Mt 14:23; 18:19; Mk 1:35; 9:29; Lk 11:1-4; 18:1 – he provided an outline of the content of our prayers Mt 6:9-15
- **Word** – Jesus knew and used the Word of God - he lived by the Word and taught his disciples to do the same Mt 4:1-11; Jn 15:7,8 – we are to spend time in the Word daily
- **Worship** – He lived a life of joy, thankfulness and dependence Mt 6:25-34; Lk 10:21; Jn 4:23. The disciples learned this lifestyle and we should follow 1Thes 5:16-19
- **Fellowship** – He depended on relationship with others – he drew aside regularly with the disciples Mt 18:20; Mk3:7; Jn 17:1,9,11,18,20,23 – strong believing friends will strengthen us
- **Witnessing** – He lived to witness to his Father and the kingdom of God Mt 4:17; 10:7; Jn 9:4; 14:10. We must witness about Jesus 1:8.

The Model of Discipling Jesus lived by these practices and trained his disciple to apply them. They became the pattern followed and taught by the disciples. When these spiritual disciplines are exercised regularly the believer will progress in relationship with Jesus becoming a disciple who 'grows and develops into a dedicated, fruitful, mature disciple who then goes on to lead others to Christ and helps them in turn as well' - Eims, Navigators.[6]

There is a great need today to help people who have come to faith in Jesus to mature in victorious living and effective ministry Gal 4:19; Heb 5:11-14. This needs to be proclaimed from the pulpit. There are many well proven programs for building disciples.[6]

Small Group Ministry The new believers met regularly in small groups particularly in homes to practice these spiritual disciplines where they were nourished and taught. This is the best means of discipling - *the things you have heard me say in the presence of many witnesses entrust to reliable men who will also be qualified to teach others 2Tim 2:2* - this is the principle of multiplication. No group is too small for this purpose Mt 18:20 – in fact the smaller the better!

Every member of the church should be involved in a small group to grow in faith and become an encourager of others. Small groups develop disciples, leaders and engage in outreach. They become the means of growth in the church. 'Home cell groups give every church member an opportunity to participate in the ministry of the church and to bring revival to their own neighborhood' Cho, pastor.[7]

You need other strong believers to build you up – other believers need you to build them up Pro 27:17; Heb 10:24,25.

The Lord added daily v47 We must always remember that we are involved in the Lord's work and ultimately it is his sovereign choice v39. When we faithfully apply the spiritual disciplines God adds the numbers.

Keys to successful ministry - there are two further aspects of the early church that need to be recognized -

• **First Love** - The believers were filled with the joy of knowing Jesus and the freedom from the burden of sin. This is the experience of all who commit their lives to Jesus as Savior and Lord. However, neglect of the spiritual disciplines and the distractions of daily living cause many to loose their zeal 1Thes 5:16-19. Jesus warned against this loss of first love Rev 2:4-6

• **Unity** - There was a common focus among the believers - they were committed to the cause of reaching others for Jesus as their primary goal. Our focus always dictates our direction and effort. It was the prayer of Jesus that disciples of his would be one, even as he is one with the Father Jn 17:20-23. This was required so that the world may believe that the Father has sent Jesus - the goal for which we are called to bear witness to him v21. The fragmentation of the church is a major hindrance to the spread of the Gospel and requires that we respond to the prayer of Jesus - for there the LORD bestows his blessing - even life forevermore Ps 133:1-3; Phil 2:1-5. Our common task must transcend our contrived differences and personalities.

The Word of God - The 'Word' included the Scriptures and the teaching of Jesus and his whole way of life Mt 4:4; Jn 1:1,14. Jesus taught the disciples from the Word and explained how it applied to their lives and circumstances Lk 24:44,45. Peter's message was based on the Word v17,25,34. The Word of God now incorporates the Gospels, Book of Acts and the Epistles.

THE EARLY CHURCH IN JERUSALEM AD 31 (3:1 to 7:60)

3:1 **The Time of Prayer** Peter and John went to the regular time of corporate prayer at the Temple. Prayer is important in the daily life of the church and of the individual. Corporate prayer is of special significance - Jesus promised to be present and to answer unified requests Mt 18:18-20.

3:2-10 **Healing a Cripple** This was a normal activity, attending the time of prayer and Peter acted spontaneously on the leading of the Holy Spirit. He offered what he had – faith in the name of Jesus. The lame man responded and was healed. He went walking, jumping and praising God – Oh the joy of serving Jesus!

In the Name of Jesus v6 Before leaving them Jesus had told the disciples - *All authority in heaven and on earth has been given to me Mt 28:18*. As a result of the sacrifice of the Son of God - *God exalted him to the highest place and gave him the name that is above every name that at the name of Jesus every knee should bow Phil 2:9,10* -

• **It is in the authority and power of his name** that Jesus told the disciples to go and make disciples Mt 28:18-20

• **It is in the authority of his name** that we have access to the Father and answers to our prayers Heb 10:19,20; Jn 14:13,14; 15:16; 16:23,24,26

• **There is power in the name of Jesus** to forgive and power to save from sin

• **There is power in the name of Jesus** to heal from sickness and power to deliver from evil.

We must realize, as Peter did, that all we do for the kingdom is done in the power and authority **of the matchless name of Jesus** Mk 16:15-18.

Miracles The occurrence of miraculous healings and events is beyond the scope of human explanation. Many have had such experiences which they regard as beyond dispute. Science cannot exclude the Creator from the laws he instituted and maintains. It is natural for people to turn to the miraculous when they have exhausted human resource.

Acts of the Apostles

We must look for and expect the intervention of God in our daily lives. This is the essential requirement for faith – *anyone who comes to him (God) must believe that he exists and that he rewards those who earnestly seek him* Heb 11:6.

Jesus promised that miracles would continue to occur – *I tell you the truth, anyone who has faith in me will do what I have been doing. He will do even greater things than these, because I am going to the Father Jn 14:11-14.* These blessings are not for our comfort, but to assist in the ministry we are called to undertake - in fact our limitations are there to allow God's power to be revealed in us 2Cor 12:9. Jesus explained that these signs would accompany the proclamation of the Gospel as a confirmation to the unbeliever - *these signs will accompany those who believe Mk 16:17.* It is characteristic of human nature that many are skeptical about matters of faith because belief requires commitment.

3:11-26 Peter's second sermon

The unexpected healing of the lame man caused excitement and a crowd. Peter challenged the people for they had joined in the call to crucify Jesus. He told them -

• God was glorifying his servant Jesus by this miracle v13
• they, the people, had disowned Jesus even though he was found to be innocent v13; Mt 27:22-26
• Jesus is the Holy and Righteous One, the author of life v14,15
• God raised Jesus from the dead and the disciples were witnesses of this fact v15
• it was by faith in the name of Jesus that the lame man was healed v16
• God was fulfilling his plan of salvation that required Jesus to suffer v18
• the people were encouraged to repent and then to return to God so that their sins may be wiped out, obliterated – both the record and the penalty v19; Col 2:14
• this was foretold by all the prophets in the Scriptures v22,24
• God was also fulfilling his Covenant promise to Abraham v25; Gen 12:3
• Jesus will return in the end time to make all things new v21 - this refers to the Great Day of the Lord when Jesus returns as judge 2:19,20; Mt 24:30; Rev 6:17.

The fact of the crucifixion and resurrection were the central theme of Peter's message v15.

Servant v13,18; 4:30 The disciples referred to the 'Suffering Servant' prophecies of Isaiah to confirm that Jesus is the Messiah Is 42:1-9; 49:1-7; 50:4-10; 52:13 to 53:12. Just as the Jewish people had difficulty in seeing the Messiah as a servant so the disciples struggled with the teaching of Jesus that he had come to be a servant Mk 10:44; Phil 2:5-8.

Today leaders in all walks of life have difficulty with being the servant of all, but this is the approach to successful management.

Jesus made it clear that we are to follow in his footsteps in serving others Mt 20:24-28; Jn 13:12-17 – *just as the Son of Man did not come to be served, but to serve and to give his life as a ransom for many Mt 20:28.*

3:14 **Holy and Righteous One** Also central to the new community was the whole new ethical standard introduced by Jesus. The Ten Commandments received by Moses remain a basis code for human behavior which is without peer in the modern world. But up to the time of Jesus the world was dictated by ruthless nations and leaders. Authority was maintained by corruption, domination and self-centeredness and without absolute values.

Jesus transformed the moral values of the world. He brought a greater understanding of the nature and character of God. He came to fulfill the Law, not by changing it but by revealing the true spirit of the Law Mt 5:17. He turned the standards of the world upside down in the Sermon on the Mount Mt 5:1-16. By his example and teaching he spoke justice for the poor and mercy for the disadvantaged. He required integrity and responsibility for leaders. He taught humility and personal commitment in all areas of life and elevated the status of women. He defined the Law as love for God and neighbor Mt 22:37-40. This love is *as I have loved you Jn 13:34,35* – love based on the self giving love of God, independent of object or response. This love was later described by Paul as the core of Christian behavior 1Cor 13:4-13. It contrasts with the sinful human nature which has its ultimate expression in evil Gal 5:19-21.

The ability to apply this standard was made possible by the indwelling presence of the Holy Spirit and appears in the life of the individual as the 'fruit of the Spirit' Gal 5:22-25 (ref p84).

The believers were committed to this new Way of life 9:2; 16:17; 18:25,26; 22:4; 24:14,22; Jn 14:6. The Christian ethic introduced by Jesus changed society over a period of time resulting in the laws and principles of the western world which are still prominent today. They are sadly under threat of diminution by liberal consensus, moral relativism and postmodern culture.

Christian institutions have suffered greatly both in experience and reputation because of the inability or unwillingness to apply the guidelines set by Jesus Mt 5:48. There is a great need for every believer to return to the way of the Lord.

4:1-7 Early Persecution – One might have expected that more of the religious leaders would consider the facts of the Gospel following the prophecies, the resurrection of Jesus and the miraculous healing of the man crippled from birth, which everybody in Jerusalem knew v16! Jn 3:1-3; 20:38-40. But the same antagonism towards Jesus was now directed at the disciples. People are often actively opposed to events and truths that impact on their lifestyles despite the facts involved. For this they will be accountable

Peter and John were arrested by the religious leaders because they were proclaiming that Jesus had risen from the dead. They were both arrested as they were each involved in the preaching. They were taken to appear before the Sanhedrin.

Sanhedrin - The Supreme Jewish Council and Court with wide but limited self-government under the Roman governor particularly in matters relating to Jewish Law and Customs. It was one of three controlling bodies along with Rome and the Herodians (supporters of the Idumaean puppet rulers and sympathizers with Rome). They were charged with maintaining the local peace.

The Sanhedrin comprised some 70 members Num 11:16 -

• **Sadducees** - of the priestly line including the current and past high priests Annas AD 6-15 and Caiaphas AD 18-36 and priestly families v6. They were wealthy aristocrats who controlled the priesthood and Temple by collaboration with Rome. Their focus was on the Temple ritual. They were conservative, supporting only the Torah, the five Books of the Law and denying tradition, the resurrection and afterlife. To them religion had become an end in itself.

• **Pharisees** - 'separate ones' - strict keepers of the Law of Moses. Apart from the Ten Commandments there were 614 commandments counted in the Torah and many others were developed to avoid breaking them. They also upheld the oral or traditional law by which the commandments could be interpreted. Jesus condemned them for their legalism and outward show Mt 23:2-4. Their main influence was in the synagogues which originated in the Babylonian exile where they had rescued the worship and strict adherence to the Law. They now kept the synagogue practices and retained their position of privilege and security by compromise with the Jewish nobility.

• **Scribes** - scholars and lawyers who were responsible for preserving the written law. The Torah, also called the Books of Moses, contained the Law of Sinai and the early history of the Hebrew people. Because the Torah was so important to daily life and knowledge it was necessary for the Scribes to explain the meaning to the people. They saw themselves as replacing the prophets of the Old Testament.

Nicodemus and Joseph of Arimathea were both Pharisees and members of the Sanhedrin who had privately come to accept the claims of Jesus as the Messiah Mk 15:43; Jn 3:1-8.

Reaction The message of the resurrection of Jesus upset the religious leaders who were being held responsible by the disciples for the execution of Jesus. They were accountable to the Romans and would maintain the peace in Jerusalem at all costs for fear of losing their privileges and religious traditions. The Sadducees were also offended because they did not accept the resurrection from the dead.

4:8-22 Peter's Third Sermon

Peter preached boldly under arrest – he was again filled with the Holy Spirit v8 -

• he declared that the healing of the lame man occurred due to the power of the name of Jesus Christ of Nazareth v10

• he reminded the leaders that they had crucified Jesus but that God had raised him from the dead v10

• *salvation is found in no one else for there is no other name under heaven given to men by which we must be saved v12.*

This was a bold statement because the religious leaders considered that it was necessary to fulfill all the requirements of the Law. It also presented the uniqueness of the salvation offered through faith in Jesus.

Time with Jesus The leaders were surprised at the courage and eloquence of Peter and John, being unlearned Galilean fishermen – *they took note that these men had been with Jesus v13.* As we spend time with Jesus, in fellowship, prayer and reading his Word we too will be transformed to be like him and empowered to serve him.

Nothing they could say v14-17 The leaders made no attempt to challenge the claims of Peter regarding the crucifixion or resurrection of Jesus or the basis for salvation. The presence of the man who was healed and standing in their presence was greater proof than they could raise to deny the claims v14. They could only hope to stop the truth from spreading v16,17.

This situation faces people today – the reality of the life and claims of Jesus are evident – they can only be resisted or embraced.

The disciples were told not to speak about Jesus. They replied that they must obey God - *we can't help speaking about what we have seen and heard v18-20.*

4:12 No other name The first disciples were convinced of the uniqueness of their message. This was explained by Jesus during his ministry – *I am the way and the truth and the life. No one comes to the Father except through me Jn 14:6.* It was demonstrated by his death and resurrection from the dead. No other philosophy of mankind makes such a claim or offers such a Savior. For this reason each person must make a decision about Jesus, to accept him or reject him 28:31.

4:23-31 The Power of Prayer When released from prison Peter and John reported to the brethren who had been praying for them. They *raised their voices together in prayer to God v24* -

• they acknowledged God's sovereign control over everything in all creation v24

• their prayer was based on the Word of God v25

• they recognized that they should expect persecution from the world in response to sharing the Gospel v26; Ps 2:1,2

• they understood that the events were proceeding according to the predetermined plan and will of God v28

• they asked for great boldness to speak the Word v29

• they asked for miracles in the name of Jesus to confirm the spoken Word, as he had promised v30; Mk 16:15-20.

As a result *they were all filled with the Holy Spirit and spoke the Word of God boldly* – we can expect this response in answer to our bold and fervent prayer v31; Jas 5:16-18.

Prayer amongst the brethren is one of the fundamental requirements for revival - 'I am persuaded that the means blessed of God to create and carry on the revival in most places, if not all, is PRAYER. You can trace its origin and progress, in every locality, to prayer." - Phillips, Welsh Revival.[8]

As well as prayer, there is also a need for courage, direction and wisdom in our witness today.

4:32-35 **Individual Commitment** All the believers were one in heart and mind – as a result great power was evident in their lives - *they continued to testify to the resurrection of the Lord Jesus and much grace was upon them all v33*. They were liberated from their fears and burdens and were living in expectation of the imminent return of Jesus. Their unity was confirmation of the presence of the Holy Spirit. Sadly this unity and power has been lost in and between many groups today Eph 4:1-5. Revival is associated with unity of the believers Ps 133:1-3.

The imminent return of Jesus From the beginning the disciples spoke about the Second Coming of Jesus - 1:10,11; 2:17; 3:19-21; 10:42,43; 17:31; 23:6; 24:21.

They had been taught by Jesus to expect his imminent return – that he will come again and when least expected - Mt 24:30,31,36-51; 25:1-13; Mk 13:32-37; Lk 12:13-21,35-40.

It is a common theme in the Epistles -
- We eagerly await a Savior Phil 3:20,21; 1Thes 5:1-3
- While we wait for the blessed hope Tit 2:12,13
- He will appear a second time – to bring salvation to those who are waiting for him Heb 9:28
- The Lord's coming is near – the Judge is standing at the door Jas 5:8,9
- The day of the Lord will come like a thief 2Pet 3:8-10
- This is the last hour 1Jn 2:18,28; 3:1-3; Rev 1:7
- See, the Lord is coming – to judge everyone Jude 1:14,15
- Behold I come like a thief Rev 16:15; 22:12, 20

John was the last of the writers around AD 90 and the vision he received left no doubt that the believer must live in anticipation of the return of Jesus and at any moment Rev 19:11-16.

We also should live in expectation of the imminent return of Jesus. What kind of people ought we to be – as we look forward to the day of God and speed its coming 2Pet 3:11-13.

4:36,37 **Barnabas** called Joseph, was a Levite of priestly descent from Cyprus. He contributed to the fellowship of believers and was given the name Barnabas (encourager) v36. He was related to Mary, mother of **John Mark** 12:12; Col 4:10 and would have a significant impact on the early church -

- he befriended and discipled Saul who became Paul the apostle to the Gentiles 9:26,27
- he launched Paul on his first mission journey 13:1-3
- he discipled Mark who became an assistant to Peter and Paul and the author of the Gospel of Mark 15:39
- he discipled the church at Antioch and at Cyprus 11:22-26

You must recognize your potential in God! You may not know the result of the things the Holy Spirit leads you to do – but you need to respond. Your few loaves and fishes placed in the hands of Jesus can meet the needs of a multitude Mt 14:16-18.

Church Growth

5:1-11 Willful deceit against God must be punished - as in the case when Israel entered the new land under Joshua and progress of the conquest was impeded until the sin of Achan had been addressed Jos 7:10,13. We must be serious about our commitment and walk with the Lord.

5:12-16 **Many signs, wonders and healings** occurred in response to their boldness and commitment. These things had been promised by Jesus to accompany the preaching of the Good News Mk 16:15-18.

While we have the reports centered on Peter and John we see here that all the apostles were involved in proclaiming the message and in the miracles v12. As well as house meetings they held public meeting daily in the Temple precincts. While some people were reluctant to join them out of fear, many more came to believe in Jesus.

This is the first use in Acts of 'church' to denote the 'assembly of the called' v11; Mt 16:18; Eph 1:22; 5:23.

Transformed lives As the first disciples were impacted by the resurrection of Jesus, the power of the Gospel changed the lives of those who subsequently accepted Jesus as Savior and Lord. This transformation has continued in the lives of countless people in all generations and from all walks of life. This is further evidence of the ongoing presence of God at work with all who will seek to acknowledge him.

5:17-28 **JERUSALEM Further Persecution** With all the positive response from the people the religious leaders were filled with envy and all of the apostles were arrested. During the night an angel released them from the prison. Next day when the full number of the Sanhedrin was assembled to put them on trial they found all of the apostles in the Temple courts preaching since daybreak motivated by joy and the Holy Spirit! They were driven by their 'first love' Rev 2:4. Their common theme was *the full message of this new life v20.*

They were re-arrested and brought before the Sanhedrin again. The charge was: **you have filled Jerusalem with the name of Jesus** – this was as requested by Jesus! They had fulfilled the first stage of Jesus' command v28; 1:8.

5:29-32 Peter's Fourth Sermon

• the reply to the charge, on behalf of all the disciples was – *we must obey God rather than men! v28,29.*
• Jesus had been crucified by the leaders as they well knew v30
• the resurrection of Jesus was the centre of the message v30
• God exalted Jesus to his own right hand as Prince and Savior
• repentance of sins was required v31
• forgiveness of sins was now possible and would be given v31
• they were witnesses of these things and so is the Holy Spirit through the boldness, miracles and changed lives v30
• the Holy Spirit is given to those who obey him v32; Gal 5:25.

Peter's reference to the 'tree' referred to the cross - an implement of shame, punishment and death introduced by the Romans around 150 BC which was transformed by Jesus into a symbol of love and hope Deu 21:23; Gal 3:13.

5:32 Response to the Holy Spirit We need to take note of the requirement for obedience and response to the Holy Spirit. Some seek blessing for their own confirmation and wellbeing - the Holy Spirit comes to empower for witness and service. Rather than looking to God for blessing in our lives we should seek to understand what God wants to do with us! We learn to get in step with what the Holy Spirit is doing in our life, our neighborhood and the world Gal 5:24,25.

5:33-41 Suffering for the name of Jesus The Council members were antagonistic - as many people are today. We must be aware that we will suffer for our outspoken faith Mt 16:24. Believers around the world are persecuted for their faith.

Gamaliel was a highly respected Pharisee and teacher (Rabbi) who had taught Paul as a Pharisee 22:3. He gave wise and prophetic advice which saved the apostles from death – *if it is from God, you will not be able to stop these men: you will only find yourself fighting against God v33.*

23   Acts of the Apostles

The apostles were flogged and told not to speak about Jesus again. They were released and rejoiced that they could suffer for the sake of the Lord. We can expect that our faith will be tested and we will meet opposition when we are committed to doing what God asks us to do - *in fact, everyone who wants to live a godly life in Christ Jesus will be persecuted 2Tim 3:12.* However this will result in joy and the power to continue with the task v41. We also can learn to rejoice in suffering 1Thes 5:16-19 - we will be overjoyed when his glory is revealed 1Pet 4:12,13.

5:42 **Day After Day** As we take every opportunity to witness to Jesus we too will experience the joy of Jesus Jn 15:11. The victorious walk comes when we apply the spiritual disciplines daily both on a personal basis and with others. As we continue to pray, appropriate the Word of God, give thanks in all circumstances, fellowship and witness to Jesus - the Holy Spirit will fill us afresh and use us in the kingdom. The God of hope will fill us with all joy and peace as we continue to believe in him so that we will abound, overflow with hope, through the power of the Holy Spirit Rom 15:13. This filling of the Holy Spirit should be the normal ongoing experience of the believer's daily walk Eph 5:17-21.

6:1-7 **Appointment of Deacons** The followers were all disciples as commanded by Jesus - *therefore go and make disciples Mt 28:19.* Today many would prefer to see a distinction between 'disciple' and 'Christian' in order to experience the blessing without the commitment! The deep joys come when we commit all our heart, soul, mind and strength Mk 12:30.

When conflict occurred the task of appointing deacons to administrate was delegated to the brethren.

The primary task of the apostles was recognized as being to *give our attention to prayer and the ministry of the Word v2-4.*

It is the recorded testimony of those who have experienced revival that the Lord responds to the persevering prayers of his people when unified across the body of believers. "Prayer meetings have been, however, the principal means with us of awakening the churches. In many places union prayer meetings (across denominations) have been very useful in drawing the public mind towards the great question of salvation - prayer, faith in God's Word, singleness of purpose, earnestness and perseverance never fail of their objective at the throne of grace; God may be nearer to us than we sometimes dare to believe" Phillips, Welsh Revival.[8]

The qualities for selection The deacons were to be full of the Holy Spirit, faith and wisdom v3. Similar qualities are given in Ex 18:21. Using these principles the number of disciples increased. The same selection criteria must apply today if we are to achieve the same results.

The appointment of seven deacons with Greek names shows the extent to which the church fellowship had grown to incorporate people of non-Jewish birth. This was in preparation for the spread of the Gospel to the Gentile world v5.

6:8-15 Stephen's Witness Stephen, one of the new deacons, empowered with the Holy Spirit, went beyond his duty of administration - he worked wonders and spoke with wisdom, engaging in discussion with non-believers. God will always use someone who is fully committed to him and prepared to step out in faith.

He was brought before the Sanhedrin because he was working outside of their jurisdiction and control. He was also undermining their authority and teaching v12.

7:1-53 Stephen's Sermon The defense given by Steven to the false charge against him was to make a direct challenge to the religious authorities.

The Messiah has come - the Promise is fulfilled! Stephen took the opportunity to preach the Gospel to the leaders - his deliberate focus was that by crucifying Jesus they had rejected the Messiah -

• he began his defense by referring to the Scriptures and the history with which they were familiar v2

• the God of Glory had appeared to Abraham in Ur of the Chaldeans – Stephen clearly saw the Gospel as relating to the call to Abraham out of polytheism by the one true God

• he went back to the promise God made about the Promised Land v3

• he emphasized the need for the promise of God to be accepted resulting in the nation of Israel v4-8

• Joseph, God's chosen one was rejected by the patriarchs (his brothers) v9

• Moses was rejected when he tried to deliver the people v27

• Moses foretold the promise of the Messiah to whom the people must listen v37 - *The LORD your God will raise up for you a prophet like me - you must listen to him Deu 18:15,18,19.* This is just one of some 300 prophetic statements that make up the promise of a future Savior and king

• Moses who received the Law at Mt Sinai was rejected by the people v39

- David and Solomon had wanted a Temple in which the people now put so much trust but God wanted obedience v48-51
- now that the Messiah, Jesus, had come they, the current leaders had rejected him - they had betrayed and murdered him v52.

7:54 The Promise Rejected The religious leaders clearly understood the point of Stephen's message - it so infuriated them that they responded violently. This is often the response of those who will not accept the truth. This incident was most significant because in condemning Stephen's message they were rejecting the 'Promise' of Jesus, the Messiah, and the gift of salvation - just like their fathers v51.

The Gospel to the Gentiles The people of Israel were known as Jews from the time of the southern state of Judah and the subsequent captivity in Babylon. The Jewish people were particularly exclusive in their beliefs. They saw themselves as separate from the ways and practices of the other nations. All non Jews were regarded as Gentiles - Romans, Greeks and other nationalities. The first believers were Jews or foreigners who had accepted the Jewish faith. They remained within the Jewish culture until the incident of Peter with Cornelius and his report to the Jerusalem Council 11:1-18. However from the time of the death of Stephen and the rejection by the religious leaders of his message the Gospel would be proclaimed as well to the Gentiles and to the world - this was according to God's plan Mt 28:18-20. God chose a deacon to bring this challenge to the leaders!

7:55-58 The Martyrdom of Stephen Because of his message Stephen was stoned to death. The ferocity of the attack was due to the directness of his accusation. It was his vision that caused them increased anger - *I see heaven open and the Son of Man standing at the right hand of God v55.*

As they had rejected the prophets and crucified the Righteous One v52 they now killed the messenger v58. God sometimes requires the ultimate sacrifice. The power and presence of the Holy Spirit was evident in the miraculous signs and preaching of Stephen as well as in his gracious and courageous acceptance of suffering and death v55,60.

Saul, a Pharisee gave assent to the execution of Stephen! v57,58. He would have been greatly impacted by the logic and wisdom of Stephen's message based as it was on the Scriptures and Traditions of the Jews. The conviction over Stephen's death remained with Saul throughout his life 22:20; 1Cor 15:9.

7:59,60 **Forgive them** We see in Steven the transformation of the human soul through the love of Jesus - *Lord, do not hold this sin against them v60.* We also see the peace and eternal assurance that come from commitment to Jesus as Savior and Lord.

THE CHURCH SCATTERED AD 32 (8:1 to 9:31)

8:1-3 **JUDEA and SAMARIA** The death of Stephen began *a great persecution* by the Jewish leaders against the believers, particularly Gentiles. Conflict often follows the proclamation of the Gospel of peace and shows the antagonism of the evil one. This persecution resulted in the believers being *scattered throughout Judea and Samaria* – the apostles remained in Jerusalem v1. Persecution was necessary to move the church out of Jerusalem 1:8. We must recognize persecution as part of God's plan. It is the response to rejection of the Gospel and evidence of judgment Jn 15:20. The church throughout the world also grows in the face of persecution. This persecution activated the next two stages of the command of Jesus to take the Gospel in all Judea and Samaria 1:8. This had all taken place within three years of the resurrection!

Saul began to destroy the church v3 Persecution is sometimes the beginning of conviction and acceptance. Saul (Hebrew) was later named Paul (Greek) 13:9.

Those who had been scattered preached the Word wherever they went v4. May we be faithful in telling others about Jesus wherever we are.

8:4-13 **Philip in Samaria** Philip, one of the seven deacons 6:5 is a model of discipleship - responding to the leading of the Holy Spirit - witnessing, preaching, taking the Word, working miraculous signs, leading people to Jesus, even baptizing them. There was hostility between the Jews and Samaritans. Perhaps Philip was in Samaria fleeing from the persecution in Jerusalem. But the presence of the Holy Spirit in him caused him to talk to the foreigners about Jesus. He preached the same message he had heard from the disciples - *proclaiming the Christ* - crucified, raised from the dead, forgiving sin - Savior and Lord v5; 2:14-41. The Holy Spirit provided the same response from the Samaritan people who heard - many accepted Christ and were baptized v12.

This confirmed the words of Jesus - *I, when I am lifted up from the earth will draw all men to myself Jn 12:32,33.* This same response will occur today when we proclaim Christ.

8:14-25 **Peter and John in Samaria** The first disciples considered the Gospel was only for Jews who accepted Jesus as Messiah – they remained within the Jewish culture. They did not see the Gospel applying to Gentiles and so were surprised at the events in Samaria. They sent Peter and John, the key evangelists to investigate v14. This was the beginning of the acceptance by the apostles that the Gospel applied as well to the people of the world 11:18; 15:12-18. Peter and John confirmed that the Samaritans had received salvation by laying hands on them - they were filled with the Holy Spirit.

Acceptance of the Samaritans was also influenced by the actions of Jesus Jn 4:39-42.

Samaritans – Samaria was located some fifty km north of Jerusalem and became the capital of the northern kingdom of Israel 1Kin 16:24. When conquered by Assyria 722 BC many of the local people, particularly the leaders, were deported to Mesopotamia. People from foreign countries were imported to repopulate the city to break up the ethnic cohesion 2Kin 17:24-29. They intermarried with the local people and came to bear the name 'Samaritan'. There was conflict with the Jews who returned to Jerusalem from the exile in Babylon 538 BC which continued to the time of Jesus and the disciples. Jesus was above this conflict and embraced the Samaritans Jn 4:4-7, 40-42. He particularly included Samaria in the field of mission 1:8.

8:26-39 **Philip and the Ethiopian** After his work in Samaria Philip was led by the Holy Spirit to go to **Gaza** some 100 km to the south where he was used in the conversion of the Ethiopian Treasurer resulting in the establishing of a Christian nation v26. We should expect the leading of God's Spirit and be prepared to respond even though at times we may not understand the full implication. It is usually when we step out in faith that we see the power of God at work in others.

Philip was able to lead the Ethiopian to Jesus from the Old Testament v35; Is 53:7,8. We must understand the power of the Word of God and be able to apply it 2Tim 2:15. We need to share God's Word rather than the wisdom and eloquence of mankind in our witnessing, teaching and preaching.

The Ethiopian was baptized in water by the side of the road v36. In all of these events with Philip and foreign people the impact of the Holy Spirit on the people responding was confirmation of the universal application of the Gospel.

Philip was then led by the Holy Spirit north to Azotus.

8:40 **Philip in Caesarea** Philip travelled north along the Mediterranean coast sharing the Gospel as he went.

Philip took up residence in Caesarea and may have been responsible for establishing the church in that city. He entertained Paul's group when they passed through. Philip had four prophetic daughters 21:8,9.

The leading of the Holy Spirit is available in our daily lives - this is an integral part of our walk with the Lord. The Spirit will lead us in the same way if we respond.

9:1-19 **The Conversion of Saul** The Gospel had now spread through Samaria to **Damascus**, a major inland Gentile city in Syria 200 km north of Jerusalem, no doubt due to the persecution. Saul in his zeal, headed there with authority from the Sanhedrin to persecute what he did not understand - the believers. Perhaps believers were known by 'the Way' even at this early stage 4:12; Jn 14:10.

The Damascus Road This pivotal event involved an appearance of Jesus who revealed himself to Saul as a light from heaven. Many have a dramatic conversion – others make a quiet personal decision in their heart. Whatever the way, it is necessary that we do make a conscious decision to embrace Jesus as Savior and follow him as Lord Jn 1:12,13; 3:3. The vision that appeared to Saul was dramatic - *who are you, Lord?* His life was changed in an instant v3-6; 26:16. Saul had approved the execution of Stephen 7:58. Now he would be used by God as an ambassador v15. He was about to see that the eternal God uses love and compassion rather than the ways of hate, conflict, persecution and domination.

Jesus explained *this man is my chosen instrument to carry my name before the Gentiles and Israel v15.*

Paul's Credentials (Paul was the Gentile name 13:9) Saul was a Hebrew of the tribe of Benjamin Phil 3:4-6, a zealous Pharisee who strictly upheld the tradition of the Jews. Son of a Pharisee 23:6, in his mid 30's, educated by Gamaliel 5:34 he was thoroughly trained in the law of the Jewish fathers. Grounded in the strict nationalism of Judaism, he was possibly a member of the Sanhedrin 8:1; 26:10 and was committed to persecuting the church 22:4,5; Gal 1:13.

Born in Tarsus, Cilicia on the south coast of Asia Minor, a cosmopolitan city of great learning and commerce, he was a Roman citizen by birth and acquainted with the Greco-Roman secular authoritarianism, culture and language 21:39; 22:3,26-28.

Familiar with both Jewish and Roman worlds he was well qualified for the task of taking the Gospel from Jerusalem to the Gentile world.

Paul's Commission *I will show him how much he must suffer for my name v16.* Paul was prepared and chosen by God and told, before undertaking ministry that he would have to suffer.

We question why we must suffer Why does evil seems to prosper over good. This is an age old issue Hab 1:2-4,12,13. Much suffering is the result of wrong decisions and bad actions by ourselves and others. We know that all things worthwhile require effort and that achievement comes through perseverance – this is a fundamental principle of the fallen world Gen 3;17-19. We all have a tendency to do wrong under certain circumstances. To do what we know to be right is often difficult. Humanistic philosophy states that there is no absolute right and wrong, only subjective values obtained by consensus.

The righteous Judge who has defined the moral standard based on his absolute character and nature in his Word will ensure that justice is ultimately established. While God provides all our needs when we place our trust in him he is more concerned with our character and who we are becoming, than with our comfort 14:22; Mt 6:33; Rom 8:28-30; Phil 4:19; Heb 5:7,9.

Obedient servant - the concerns of Ananias about assisting Saul are understandable, however his obedience to God's calling is our example v13,17.

Scales fell from his eyes v18. It is this condition of blindness that requires our patience, persistence in witnessing and prevailing prayer for unbelievers 2Cor 4:4. This is the reason for our dependence on the leading of the Holy Spirit in speaking to unbelievers. It is only the Holy Spirit who can convict of guilt, of sin and righteousness and of judgment Jn 16:8. It is only the Holy Spirit who can bring about the new birth Jn 3:5-8.

The conversion of Saul confirms the power of God and the Gospel to transform the life of the individual. He, along with the other disciples and countless others through the generations who have been born again and had nothing to gain from the world, were prepared to lay down their lives for the risen Savior.

God's sovereign choice The sovereign power and purposes of God are beyond dispute. His purpose in election is clear. He chooses whom he will and assigns them to the task for which he has raised them. Paul became very aware of this evidence of God's mercy and compassion Rom 9:14-18. He saw himself as the 'worst of sinners' having persecuted the church and condoned the death of Stephen 22:19,20; 1Tim 1:15. However we know that God is not willing that any should perish but that everyone come to repentance 2Pet 3:9. God is sovereign and mankind is responsible - these are two profound truths with which we must come to terms - we work as God wills Eph 2:10; Phil 2:12,13. An 'antinomy' refers to two truths, both found in Scripture which are beyond our human ability to reconcile Is 55:8,9. This matter of predestination and freewill is a concern for those who would limit the God of the universe to the understanding of the finite mind of mankind. However it is the source of awe, reverence and thankfulness for those who have been open to God's grace.

9:20-31 **Saul's Early Ministry** Following his conversion Saul spent some days with the disciples in Damascus – those who he had come to persecute. His bold and brilliant testimony and preaching brought objection and resistance from the Jewish leaders. As a Pharisee his knowledge of the Scriptures gave him a unique position to argue the truth of the Gospel. Resistance was so strong that he was caused to depart from the city by night.

Revelation in Arabia It is likely that at this time Saul spent three years in the Arabian wilderness possibly in seclusion. The challenge of the risen Christ to his pharisaic training caused him to withdraw for study of the Scriptures and meditation where he developed his deep understanding of the Gospel as part of fourteen years of preparation. There he had special revelation from Christ Gal 1:11-23 - things that were regarded as deep even for Peter 2Pet 3:15,16. We must each see our life's training as preparation for the next step in our service for the Lord.

The Hope of Israel Saul, the Pharisee came to realize that the Scriptures and the expectations of God's people were fulfilled in Jesus 23:6; 24:14,15; 26:6,7; 28:20. We must see the validity of the Old Testament in understanding our heritage in Christ Lk 24:25-27,44-48; 1Cor 10:11.

In Jerusalem When he arrived in Jerusalem the disciples there were understandably afraid to associate with him because of his reputation and his support for the death of Stephen v26; Gal 1:23. It was Barnabas, the encourager who *took him and brought him to the apostles v27*. We must always be ready to accept and encourage unlikely people who God brings across our paths. Everyone has potential before God and we may

Acts of the Apostles

not know what wonderful plan he has for their lives. He may use us to take them to the next level – this happens frequently with the one who is open to the leading of the Holy Spirit.

Saul had an effective ministry for a while but when persecution from the Jews increased the disciples sent him to Caesarea and then to his home town of Tarsus v28. This was motivated by a vision and word from the Lord 22:17. Saul became a target for fundamental Jews for the remainder of his life.

Visions It is common for believers to receive visions - guidance they accept as divine wisdom - included among the spiritual gifts as a message of knowledge (ref p85). There are a number of visions recorded in Acts -

• Saul saw a vision of Jesus which led to his conversion and changed the direction of his whole life 9:3; 9:12; 26:19

• Ananias was led to visit Saul despite his apprehension 9:12

• Cornelius, a Roman believing centurion was guided by a vision to send to Joppa for Peter 10:3

• Peter was given instructions to accept a visit to a Gentile house, both by a vision and a word of knowledge 10:17,19

• Peter explained the vision and its outworking to the Council of believers in Jerusalem 11:5-17

• Peter encountered a real experience which he took for a vision – he was actually released from prison 12:7-9

• In the midst of uncertainty Paul received a vision of a Macedonian man which changed the direction of his ministry from Asia into Europe 16:9

• Paul received encouragement about the outcome of a shipwreck 18:9

• Paul was given direction about testifying in Rome 23:11.

Apart from the Scriptures there have been countless examples of visions even in modern times to those who did not have an exposure to the gift. Some may explain these encounters as metaphysical (beyond the measurable physical world) or even as psychosomatic. However the value to the receiver and the dramatic impact on their lives confirms the reality of their experiences. It is important to test the spirits to see whether they are from God 1Jn 4:1.

We must expect the Lord to lead us and to speak to us in all manner of ways. Always confirm it by the Word of God. Then we need to step out in faith.

THE GOSPEL RECEIVED BY THE GENTILES – AD 40 (9:32 to 11:18)

9:32-43 **Local Ministry** The church grew throughout Judea, Galilee and Samaria. Peter's ministry included pastoral visits to local towns like Lydda and Joppa south of Jerusalem, teaching and healing people and even raising a woman from the dead. He stayed there for some time.

10:1-33 **The Conversion of Cornelius in Caesarea** A Roman centurion and God-fearing man had a vision in which he was told to send to Joppa for Peter. Once again we see God's sovereign purpose being worked out in advance of the plans of the leaders. At this same time Peter had an amazing series of visions in which he was told *do not call anything impure that God has made clean v15.* This prepared him for the visit to Caesarea - without the vision it would have been unacceptable for him to enter a Gentile household v27. Despite his preaching he was still inclined to see the Gospel as limited to the Jewish people. We must beware of our hidden prejudices.

While considering the vision, the men from Cornelius arrived. The Holy Spirit then led Peter to accept their invitation v19.

10:34-48 **Peter's Fifth Sermon**

Next day in Caesarea Peter came to the realization *that God - accepts men from every nation who fear him and do what is right v34.*This shows the initial reluctance and the ultimate impact of this experience.

He began to explain the Gospel to the gathering of Gentiles at the house of Cornelius - the Good News of peace with God through faith in Jesus. By now this message and the impact on the lives of people was know even in Caesarea v36,37 -

• Peter began by acknowledging Jesus as Lord of all v36

• Jesus lived life doing good, teaching, healing and delivering from evil – the 'anointing' of Jesus refers to the Messiah v38

• Peter confirmed they were witnesses to all that Jesus did v39

• He was crucified by the leaders but God raised him from the dead on the third day v40

• He appeared to many of the disciples and commanded them to preach this message v41; 1:3

• Jesus is the One whom God has appointed as judge of the living and the dead v42

• everyone who believes in him receives forgiveness of sins v43

• to this all the prophets testify v43.

The Response While he was still speaking *the Holy Spirit came on all who heard the message v44*. This was a shock to Peter's colleagues due to their Jewish focus. By this they were compelled to recognize God's intention for the Gospel to be available to all people and nations of the earth v46. Once again we see the sovereignty of God at work through the Holy Spirit. The people were baptized with water, even though they had already received the gift of the Holy Spirit v47.

11:1-18 **Back in Jerusalem** Against criticism from the Jewish brethren Peter explained his vision, his experience and his change in perspective to the other apostles v2.

As I began to speak the Holy Spirit came on them as he had come on us at the beginning v15. It was this baptism of the Holy Spirit that confirmed the new birth and convinced the believers that the Gospel was universal 8:17.

Who was I to think that I could oppose God? v17. They had no further objections and so concluded that *God has granted even the Gentiles repentance unto eternal life v18*. This means salvation is available to us!
Light for the Gentiles God's plan of salvation has always included all people Gen 12:1-3. Israel was redeemed out to Egypt to be a holy nation through whom God would show himself holy to the nations of the world Ex 19:4-6; Ezk 37:21-23. But they profaned his name by their rebellion and refusal to follow his ways and were disciplined by exile to Babylon. Isaiah, the great prophet of Judah saw that the Messiah would bring salvation to the nations and be a light to the Gentiles Is 11:10; 42:6; 49:6. This was foretold at the birth of Jesus Lk 2:28-32. After the glory of the monarchy Israel was dominated by the nations and became a proud, self-centered, insulated people who saw themselves as separate from the other nations.

While the disciples accepted the teaching of Jesus about the universal plan they had difficulty in departing from their ingrained Jewish culture. It was Paul who came to grasp the greater plan through his commission as Apostle to the Gentiles 9:15,16; 13:47; 22:21; 26:23.

It is the believer who is now called to take the message of salvation to the nations 1Pet 2:9.

THE CHURCH AT ANTIOCH AD 42 (11:19 to 12:25)

11:19-24 **The Gentile Church** The Gospel was now spreading into **Antioch** in **Syria**, on the Mediterranean Coast some 500 km north of

Jerusalem. Antioch was the capitol of the Roman province of Syria and one of the largest cities of the day. As a result of the persecution in Jerusalem the Gospel spread along the coast to Antioch among the Jews v19. Now believers came from the Island of Cyprus and Cyrene on the coast of Northern Africa and preached to the non-Jews (Gentiles) v20. *A great number of people believed and turned to the Lord v21.*

11:22-26 **Break with traditions** The apostles in Jerusalem were still adjusting to acceptance of the Gentiles. Barnabas, a Cypriot layman was sent from Jerusalem to investigate v22. On arrival he realized that the new believers at Antioch needed to be discipled in the new faith. They included many Gentiles who would have little knowledge of Jewish history or Old Testament Scriptures. Saul's knowledge of Judaism and the Greek language together with his dramatic conversion would be of great assistance in the task. So Barnabas went to Tarsus and recruited Saul to assist. He had recognized Saul's potential when he came across him in Jerusalem 9:27.

11:26 **Discipleship** It is important for believers to develop in their understanding of their faith and the Word of God. This is vital to their growth, to victorious living and to their effectiveness in sharing their faith with others. Each assembly should have an ongoing 'every member' discipleship program where experienced disciples become involved with new believers, sharing their relationship with Jesus. *So for a whole year Barnabas and Saul met with the church and taught great numbers of people v26.*
This action by Barnabas reactivated Saul's ministry.

11:26 The disciples were called Christians first at Antioch God's intention is still that Christians be disciples! 6:1; Mt 28:18,19. The term 'disciple' occurs 266 times in the Gospels and Acts, the term 'Christian' only 3 times. A disciple is a follower of Jesus, who becomes like Jesus and does what Jesus did Lk k9:23,24; 14:27; Jn 15:8. It is in commitment to Jesus and his service that joy becomes complete Jn 15:9-11.

11:27-30 **First Visit to Jerusalem** Barnabas and Saul were sent to Jerusalem as representatives of the believers in Antioch with contributions for famine relief. This occurred fourteen years after Saul's conversion Gal 2:1. It was his first official visit to the church in Jerusalem. Secular history records widespread famine in the reign of Emperor Claudius AD 41-54.

***12:1-25* Peter in Prison** Persecution continued in Jerusalem from the religious leaders and the local ruler. Herod Agrippa I AD 41-44 was puppet king of Judea and head of the Herodians, secular sympathizers with Rome. He was the grandson of Herod the Great 37-4 BC who ruled at the time of the birth of Jesus Mt 2:1. He executed James the brother of John, one of the twelve disciples, the first of many to be martyred Mt 4:21. This pleased the Jews so he imprisoned Peter.

Prevailing Prayer The church met in the home of Mary, mother of John Mark, the cousin of Barnabas. They were *earnestly praying to God for Peter v5*. As a result an angel released him so he went to the prayer meeting late at night. The believers were so surprised they did not believe it was him – they were not expecting such a quick answer to their prayer! v16. We must expect great answers to our prayers - always expect the knock on the door! Lk 18:1.

This was the last mention of Peter's ministry in Acts as the record turns to focus on world mission.

God's Judgment Apart from his evil ways Herod's pride and arrogance caused him to deny God. History confirms the date of Herod's death as AD 44 and hence the date of these events in the church v23.

The Word of God continued to spread v24.

Barnabas and Saul returned to Antioch taking John Mark, cousin of Barnabas with them v 25; 4:36,37; 12:12.

The Early Church was now established with the centre in Jerusalem presided over by the apostles and James, the brother of our Lord. The Gospel had spread throughout Jerusalem, Judea and Samaria. It now even reached the Gentiles in Syria with the new centre developing in Antioch. The scene was set for expansion *to the ends of the earth 1:8*.

THE FIRST MISSION JOURNEY AD 45 - 48 (13:1 to 15:35)
The Gospel spread during the early years in a number of ways -
• those converted while visiting Jerusalem at Pentecost had returned home 2:1-12
• many who fled the persecution took the message with them
• the disciples would have gone out to take the message 19:1
• believers from Cyprus and Cyrene in northern Africa preached in Antioch 11:19

There were many other mission journeys and adventures but the Book of Acts now centres specifically on the significant work of Saul (Paul) - for which we can be grateful for Luke.

13:1-3 **Outreach from Antioch** The leaders, prophets and teachers used the spiritual disciplines of *worshipping the Lord and fasting!* During this practice the Holy Spirit called them to commission Barnabas and Saul for mission. This was the next step in the Holy Spirit's plan!

It was to be expected that a Gentile centre outside of Jerusalem would become the hub of outreach to the world. It was unencumbered by Jewish tradition and open to receive the pure Gospel of grace through faith in Christ without works of the law.

The first mission journey took them to southern and central Asia Minor.

13:4-12 **CYPRUS** Barnabas and Saul with John Mark sailed from **Seleucia** near Antioch to the island of **Cyprus**, home of Barnabas. At **Paphos** they encountered a sorcerer who opposed them and was struck blind for a time. As a result the proconsul (governor) became a believer v12.

Saul changed his Jewish name to the Gentile name of Paul and from this time on he took the lead.

Demonic Forces For those who have been involved in assisting people experiencing the consequences of demonic forces or occult practices the spirit world is a stark reality.

There is a conflict between good and evil - outside of the realm of the natural sciences but dramatically within the experience of many. There are numerous examples of evil in leaders throughout history.

Jesus acknowledged and addressed evil. There is a realm of rulers and authorities, powers of this dark world and spiritual forces of evil in the heavenly realms against which we are called to take our stand Eph 6:10-13.

13:13 **ASIA MINOR** From **Cyprus** they sailed north to **Perga** in **Pamphylia** on the coast of mainland **Asia Minor** where the youthful John Mark left them. This was to cause future contention with Paul 15:36-40.

As they entered the cosmopolitan cities of Asia Paul's skills and zeal under God came to the fore 9:15,16.

13:14,15 **GALATIA** They travelled north to **Pisidian Antioch** in the Roman province of **Galatia**. Paul went first to the local synagogue on the Sabbath to speak to the Jews. This was to be his usual approach as it would have been easier to gain a receptive audience among the Jews. He also believed the Jews who respected the Scriptures would respond to the message and should be given the first chance to hear the Gospel. As a Jew himself he knew the love of God for the Jewish people Ezk 37:24-28; Zec 13:9. He understood that a window of opportunity had been opened up until the fullness of the Gentiles has come in and then Israel will be redeemed in the final days Rom 11:25-32.

Synagogue The local synagogues meeting for worship and the reading and teaching of the Torah originated in the Babylonian exile where the strict adherence to the Law was taught and practiced. They were controlled by the Pharisees. It was the custom to give visitors the opportunity to speak. Jesus attended the synagogue meetings as was the Jewish custom. He often spoke to the people and taught them Mt 12:9; 13:54. Paul sought a receptive audience in the synagogues. When the Temple was destroyed AD 70 the synagogue remained the focus for the Jewish faith.

13:16-41 Paul's First Recorded Sermon

As a visiting dignitary Paul was asked to speak to the gathering of Jews and Gentiles in the synagogue. He gave them the Gospel -

• he referred to God's calling of the people of Israel through the patriarchs and their deliverance from bondage in Egypt v17

• God gave them judges and prophets, then kings; first Saul, then David, a man after God's heart v22; 1Sam 13:14

• God raised the descendant of David as he promised

• this Messiah is the Savior Jesus v23; 2Sam 7:12,16

• John the Baptist announced the coming of Jesus v25

• the message of salvation through Abraham was sent to the Jewish and God-fearing people v26

• the people of Jerusalem and their rulers did not recognize Jesus as Messiah – yet they fulfilled the words of the prophets v27

• though he had done no wrong the people crucified him v29

• this was necessary to fulfill the prophecies that the Messiah should die v27

• but God raised him from the dead which the disciples witnessed v30,31

• by the resurrection of Jesus, God has fulfilled his promise to the forefathers to send a Messiah and king v32,33 –

- this acknowledgement of Jesus also confirmed the Fatherhood of God and the Sonship of Jesus v33; 3:17
- *through Jesus the forgiveness of sins is proclaimed to you v38*
- through Jesus all who believe are justified, this could not be achieved by the law of Moses v39.

Doctrine of the Early Church (ref p67) From this message the basic teaching of Paul can be established. It contains the central doctrine of the Christian faith and is consistent with the first sermon of Peter 2:14-41. The importance of the Person of Jesus and the resurrection confirming the death of Jesus as the means of forgiveness of sin is supported by quotations from the Scriptures showing that Jesus had fulfilled many of the Old Testament prophecies. Paul the Jew and expert in the Law confirmed that in raising Jesus from the dead God was fulfilling his promise of the Messiah v32,33. While Paul's later letters were to present in more detail the deep understanding of the things of God based on his education and revelation the content of the early messages of the apostles contain all things necessary for salvation and effective witnessing. Paul acknowledged that he had received the basic message from the first disciples 1Cor 15:3-8.

The Grace of God v32 Having being freed from the binding conditions of the law and finding forgiveness for his persecution of the church Paul was overcome by the grace of God v38,39. He was *justified from everything you could not be justified from by the law of Moses v39*. This was a personal testimony. He would refer to this grace at the beginning of every one of his letters and throughout his preaching Rom 1:7; 2Cor 8:9; Titus 3:4-7. Grace is a revealed attribute of God. It is the free, unmerited, undeserved, unlimited favor of the loving Heavenly Father and is available to all who accept Jesus as Savior and Lord. He paid the price on Calvary to make this grace available. God's grace, like his love is not due to the response but to the source.

When the time had fully come v33; Gal 4:4 Paul also saw that God was fully in control of the affairs of mankind and that he was intervening at the right time - *what God promised our fathers he has fulfilled for us v33*. If Jesus was born 70 years earlier there was no peace - 70 years later there was no Temple (or Jerusalem). A number of strategic conditions were in place -
- The Greek Hellenistic culture was promoted by Alexander 336-323 BC. After 200 years of domination the Greek language with its richness

and wide flexible vocabulary was common throughout the civilized world - the local language of Palestine was Aramaic 22:2

• Rome now had control of Palestine from 63 BC and ruled the know world with a strict form of organization, law and justice that remained for 400 years. The emperor Augustus 27 BC-14 AD had established a reign of peace and stability with extensive military roads throughout the empire which provided communications, ease of mobility and travel around the known world

• Contemporary philosophy and religion had failed. The great thinkers had not achieved their goals. The combination of many Greek and Roman gods had failed to bring unity. There was a longing for answers to the questions of life

• Materialism and self-indulgence led to a decline in morals and people were looking for meaning to life

• Despite the rule of law the moral standard was abused and the conduct of leaders and the people was corrupt and self-promoting

• The Jews had returned to their homeland and restored the Temple worship, Law and Traditions but had failed to gain independence – their religion had become formal and impersonal

• Jewish communities were scattered through the world from the dispersion providing a contact base for spreading the message

• Zealots, terrorists, plotted against the occupation of Rome advocating active violence and resistance

• The Jewish people were looking forward to the prophesied Messiah who they expected would deliver them from oppression, overthrow Rome and bring about God's new universal kingdom

• So people gave ready response to the actions and teaching of Jesus.

By God's providence these were the right conditions for the spread of the Gospel to the world - as acknowledged by all 2:23; 4:28; 7:17. This is further evidence of God's involvement in the universe and the affairs of his people.

13:42-49 **Gospel for the Gentiles** Paul's message raised great interest among the people. They were asked to speak again on the next Sabbath and a large crowd assembled. But the Jews took offence, mainly out of jealousy rather that at the content of the message. The divide between Christians and Jews would grow.

We had to speak the Word of God to you first - since the Jewish leadership rejected the Gospel Paul declared that they would *now turn to the Gentiles v46*.

Paul was quick to see that the lack of response from the Jews confirmed his commission to be *a light for the Gentiles v47*; 22:21.

Many Gentiles did believed - *all who were appointed for eternal life v48*. From now on Gentile response would characterize the success of their ministry.

13:50-52 Persecution The Jews incited opposition, a common response of those who are antagonistic to the beliefs of others. Those who believed became disciples and were filled with joy and with the Holy Spirit.

14:1-7 Iconium They moved east to Iconium in Galatia where many Jews and Gentiles believed. Some Jews spoke against Paul. They stayed to teach and many miracles confirmed the Word that was spoken. The city was divided and a plot to stone them was discovered so they moved south to **Lystra** where they continued to preach v7.

14:8-19 Lystra A cripple was cured when Paul *saw that he had faith to be healed v9*. As a result the crowd considered Paul and Barnabas to be representatives of the Greek gods and planned to make sacrifice to them v11,12.

Then Jews from Antioch arrived turning the crowd against Paul and so they stoned him. How fickle people can be.

14:20,21 Derbe When Paul revived, he and Barnabas left Lystra and went southeast to Derbe where many became disciples.

14:21-25 Return to Lystra, Iconium and Antioch On the return journey they strengthening the new disciples as they went. Elders were appointed in each location to administer.

14:22 Through many hardships They reflected on the trials they had faced. Paul suffered an illness while in Galatia Gal 4:13,14. He also recognized the persecution that comes from those who are not constrained by love and respect both from those who opposed the Gospel and those who defended Judaism. He recognized *we must go through many hardships to enter the kingdom of God v22*.

Paul was to provide a list of the many times of persecution, struggle and hardship he would face – in prison frequently, exposed to death frequently, five times lashed, three times beaten with rods, stoned once and shipwrecked three times – in danger from the elements, bandits,

Jews, Gentiles and even false brothers 2Cor 11:21-29. Yet he found the ability to survive and continue.

The secret of contentment Paul understood the sovereignty of God – that God is in control of every situation.

He learned to be satisfied with what God had provided and to have the will to persevere. He could *do everything through him (Jesus) who gives me strength Phil 4:11-13.* This is the assurance of Jesus to all those who put their trust in him - be anxious about nothing Mt 6:25-33. This secret of contentment is an important lesson to learn in every circumstance of life.

14:26-28 They then left Galatia and sailed back to Antioch in Syria, their home church where they reported on the success of their mission. They continued to minister at Antioch for a long time.

The Great Jerusalem Council

15:1,2 **Adding to the Gospel** While Paul and Barnabas were ministering in Antioch some **Judaizers** came from Judea. (These were people who had recognized Jesus but remained loyal to the Pharisees and wished to enforce Jewish customs on the new believers v5). They wanted to compel Gentile believers to observe Jewish laws and rituals, particularly the act of circumcision. While this was considered compulsory by the Jews it was not essential for salvation as a result of the sacrificial death of Jesus.

It may have been during this time that Peter visited Antioch and fell into dispute with Paul about this matter Gal 2:11-13.

Paul also received word at this time that the believers in the province of Galatia were being undermined by these Jewish sympathizers who were adding to the Gospel. He wrote the Epistle to the Galatians at this time in defense of his authority and teaching.

15:3-6 **Second Visit to Jerusalem** It was understandable that Jewish converts might expect to continue with their customs. But the Gentile believers had little or no knowledge of the Jewish practices. This brought into focus the issue of faith in Christ alone. It was not about setting aside the law or the moral code, but whether believers outside the Jewish faith should have to adopt Jewish customs in order to be saved.

As a result of this dispute Paul and Barnabas were appointed by the local believers to go to Jerusalem to consult the church Council.

They were welcomed by the church assembly and reported on their mission activities in Galatia and Antioch v4.

The issue of Jewish customs was raised by the Pharisee supporters v5. The church Council, consisting the apostles and elders then met where rigorous debate on this subject took place v6.

15:7-11 **Peter proclaimed** *we believe it is through the grace of our Lord Jesus that we are saved, just as they are v11* - both Jew and Gentile.

15:12 **Paul's experience** As a strict Pharisee Paul knew the bondage of being under the Law, having to obey all the requirements at all times and it was from this burden that he had been released at the feet of Jesus. He was determined to defend the cause of salvation by grace, through faith in Christ alone Rom 1:16,17.

Barnabas and Paul reported on the response to the Gospel amongst the Gentiles (the people in Galatia) where many were saved and fledgling churches had been established – this was important confirmation of God's grace v12.

15:13-21 **James** who led the Council was the son of Mary and the younger half-brother of our Lord. He did not accept the claims of Jesus until the resurrection when he became a follower - further confirmation of the deity of Jesus and the grace of God Jn 7:5.

Now he had been appointed to head the Council of apostles and elders v6,13; 12:17. He recalled the Old Testament prophecy that the Gentiles would be saved v15; Amos 9:11,12. James made the concluding judgment.

15:22-29 **Apostolic Declaration** This Council was of great importance as it established the basis for universal belief in **salvation by grace, through faith in Christ alone and not by having to fulfill works of the Law** Eph 2:8,9. It took the experience of a devout Pharisee to see the full implication of the work of Jesus.

An official letter was written by the Council with full apostolic authority and sent to the Gentile believers who were recognized as brothers. They were advised to refrain from practices associated with idol worship but no other restrictions were required. This decision meant that there is nothing that can be added to the requirements for salvation that come through faith in Jesus Christ alone – all other customs, rituals and observances where but a shadow of the reality that is found in Christ Col 2:16,17! This truth was strenuously maintained by subsequent leaders.[12]

God's Plan of Salvation

The purpose of Jesus coming to earth was to establish God's plan for the salvation of all who would turn to him in faith Jn 3:16-18. The principles of this plan were proclaimed through the prophets of old and are the central message of the teaching of the disciples from the beginning. This matter was formalized by the Council. It includes the following essential steps -

• all have sinned and fall short of the glory of God Rom 3:23
• the wages of sin is death but the gift of God is eternal life in Jesus Christ our Lord Rom 6:23
• we are justified freely because Christ died for us Rom 5:8
• we cannot save ourselves – it is the gift of God Eph 2:8,9
• when we accept Jesus as our savior and Lord we are born again through faith in Jesus by the operation of the Holy Spirit Jn 1:12,13; 1Pet 1:23.

This plan of salvation applies to all who will believe in Jesus today Is 53:1-12; Rom 2:21-31. We need to know it and accept it for ourselves. Then we need to able to share it with others.

A cosmic change took place when Jesus died. God's holiness, justice, mercy and love came together at the cross! *God presented him as a sacrifice of atonement, through faith in his blood – he did it to demonstrate his justice – so as to be just and the one who justifies those who have faith in Jesus Rom 3:25,26;* Rom 5:8.

The sin of man could be forgiven, the offense removed and eternal life made available for those who choose to accept God's Son as Savior and Lord Col 1:13,14.

The importance of this decision by the Council of believers in Jerusalem is central to the faith. There have been a multitude of diversions which have divided the church and caused loss of focus and respect. Believers throughout the body of Christ need to unite on this central and fundamental truth and proclaim it fearlessly to the world 4:12.

15:30-35 **Return to Antioch** Paul and Barnabas returned to their home church with the letter confirming the basis for salvation in Christ alone. They were accompanied by Judas and Silas, two of the church leaders who were also prophets. They remained and ministered in Antioch for a period v22,32. By this time many others had be discipled and trained to teach and preach the Word of the Lord – it is important for the church to use all recourses to the maximum benefit v35; 2Tim 2:2.

The First Mission Journey resulted in significant gains -
• the Gospel was recognized by the church as providing salvation by faith in the Lord Jesus Christ alone and not by works of the Law

- salvation through the Lord Jesus Christ was confirmed by the church as being not for the Jewish people only but also for the Gentiles, people of the world as well
- the Gospel was firmly established throughout Galatia in Asia Minor.
- Paul was recognized as a leader and apostle to the Gentiles.

Statements of Belief The basic principles of belief as established by Jesus and reinforced by his teaching in the 40 days following the resurrection are recorded in the sermons of Peter and Paul. They are expounded in the letters of the apostles - the Epistles of Paul and the General Epistles. They have been enshrined in universal statements of belief. The agreed teaching is most concisely set out in the Apostles Creed (ref p67).

THE SECOND MISSION JOURNEY AD 50 - 53 (15:36 to 18:22)

15:36-41 Paul and Barnabas considered a second journey to Galatia to check on progress with the churches they had established. A disagreement occurred over John Mark concerning his departure during the previous journey 13:13. Paul was later to recognize Mark's commitment and ability no doubt as a result of the discipling by Barnabas 2Tim 4:11; Phm 1:24. Mark also became a valuable assistant to Peter in Rome 1Pet 5:13.

Barnabas took John Mark and went to minister in Cyprus, his home country v39.

Paul and Silas returned overland to **Asia Minor** v40,41. They would then be directed to Macedonia and Greece.

Travelling through **Syria and Cilicia** (Tarsus was Paul's home) they strengthened the churches which had been commenced during the first journey.

16:1-5 GALATIA Paul and Silas went back to **Derbe, Lystra and Iconium** moving from town to town. **Timothy,** a disciple from Lystra joined the team – he was required to be circumcised to avoid conflict with the Jews. They delivered the Jerusalem Council decision. The believers they visited were strengthened.

16:6-8 NORTHERN ASIA The team moved north to new towns in the region but were kept from preaching the Word throughout Asia by the leading of the Holy Spirit! v6. Moving northwest they were again stopped from going into **Bithynia** and eventually came to **Troas** (near Troy) in **Mysia** v7. It is important to recognize the restraining influence of the Holy Spirit as well as positive guidance.

16:9,10 **EUROPE - The Macedonian Man** In Troas Paul received a night vision v9. They immediately sailed for **Macedonia**. They had been prevented from their plans because the Holy Spirit had a greater task for them – to reach Europe.

Luke recruited It was here in Troas that Luke, beloved physician, soon to be author of the Books of Luke and Acts joined Paul, together with Timothy and Silas v10.

Guidance – We can learn some of the principles of obtaining guidance from the Lord -

• First we must recognize that God does guide us. He has a plan for our lives and wants us to respond to his leading Ps 32:8; Jer 29:11-14; Jn 10:27,28

• We need to be sensitive to the leading of the Holy Spirit. This is a skill that comes with practice and application. We develop a relationship with the Lord as we walk daily with him, through exercising the spiritual disciplines 2:42-47; 10:9,15,19,20

• The witness of the Holy Spirit is vital – he not only directs us and provides our wellbeing but also prevents us as we learn to respond to his leading v6,7; 13:1-4

• The Spirit speaks in a still, small voice – as we listen and respond, this will result in a growing conviction and confirmation of the direction to take v9; 1Kin 19:9-13

• Guidance will always be in conformity with the Word of God – this is one reason why we must be familiar with God's Word by regular study, meditation and application v10

• It is good to obtain conformation by consulting other believers with whom you have developed confidence through regular fellowship 1Sam 23:16

• It is necessary to step out in faith v10-12; 2Kin 7:5-7

• Sometimes we are asked to do something we may not understand or necessarily chose to do v19-23

• Our response will require commitment and perseverance – our faith will be tested, but we will see the purpose of the Lord in blessing to others v25,34.

16:11-15 **MACEDONIA** They landed at **Neapolis** then went on to the major city of **Philippi** 18:12. On the Sabbath they went to a place of prayer where they met and spoke to a group of women.

Lydia, a business woman was converted – *the Lord opened her heart to respond v14.* She and her household were baptized and she persuaded them to *'come and stay!' v15.*

The Role of Women – Contrary to the custom of the day, women played a prominent role in the early church –

• they were among the first believers and contributed in the decision-making 1:14,15

• they were present at Pentecost and were involved in the ministry 2:1-4,17,18

• many women responded to Jesus as Savior 5:14; 17:4,34

• Dorcas was involved in hospitality ministry 9:36-43

• Mary, mother of John Mark was prominent in house group and prayer ministry 12:12

• Lydia, a business woman was first to respond to Jesus in Europe and became a leader 16:13-15,40

• Priscilla with her husband Aquila 18:2,18,26; Rom 16:3-4

• this respect for the role of women and their involvement in service was taught and demonstrated by Jesus, many of whom had been healed by him and supported his ministry.

16:16-24 **The Cost of Serving** At the place of prayer a slave girl, used as a fortune teller acknowledged the Most High God. Paul demonstrated power over the demonic – in the name of Jesus Lk 10:9; Col 2:15. Opposition led to a riot. As Paul and Silas were looking to success they were flogged and imprisoned for causing a disturbance v24.

16:25-40 **The Power of Praise** At midnight, in stocks, they were praying and singing praise to God v25. We learn to give thanks in all circumstances because this is God's will - this is the atmosphere in which the Holy Spirit operates. Our negative attitude puts out the Spirit's fire 1Thes 5:16-19.

The thanksgiving resulted in the conversion of the jailer and his family. *Believe in the Lord Jesus and you will be saved – you and your household v31.* The jailer was filled with joy v34 - this is the promise to all who will believe and is also their experience!

We can recognize that in the midst of persecution our prayer and praise can turn disaster into glory as God's power works in us.

In the morning they were released and asked to leave the city. Lydia had established a home group v40.

17:1-9 **Thessalonica** They moved west to Thessalonica also in Macedonia where Paul went to the synagogue as was his custom. He proved from the Scriptures that Jesus is Christ. Remember that the Old Testament Scriptures were the only 'Bible' the early Christians had. The New Testament we have today was still in the making. Yet they could demonstrate from the Old Testament that Jesus is the Messiah Lk 24:25-27,32,44-48. We also need to develop familiarity with the whole Word of God.

Some of the Jews and many of the Gentiles believed and became followers v4.

The strict Jews were jealous and another riot occurred. The content of Paul's message is clear – *another king, one called Jesus v7.*

17:10-15 **Berea** As a result of the conflict they moved on further west. Many became believers v10. *The Bereans were of more noble character - for they received the message with great eagerness and examined the Scriptures every day to see if what Paul said was true v11.* A noble Christian reads the Bible daily to hear from God and to confirm understanding – this leads to growth, victorious living and effectiveness in service 20:32.

Trouble followed them from Thessalonica requiring Paul to be rescued v13.

17:16,17 **GREECE** While Silas and Timothy remained at Berea to stabilize the new believers Paul was taken south to **Athens**, a city full of idols where he preached in the synagogue and marketplace daily *the good news about Jesus and the resurrection v18.*

17:18-21 **The Philosophers of the day** The early thinkers developed philosophies which are rather common in various forms and circles among people today -

Epicurus taught materialism around 300 BC - that the world is a result of random motions and particles. There was no divine intervention in life; the gods were not involved in human existence. The aim of life was pleasure, peace and freedom from fear - death was the end of existence.

Stoics About the same time the Stoics believed in reason over emotion. They saw the universe as a single organism with a world soul called 'Reason' - an impersonal force that worked throughout the universe to achieve a predetermined goal. Stoics held high moral integrity, self-sufficiency and acceptance (fate) as the purpose of life. These groups were attracted to Paul's new ideas.

After discussion they took Paul to the Areopagus Council, the philosopher's corner, to address the thinkers. The message of Jesus Christ raised from the dead, Savior of those who believe in him was new to these Greek experts v19.

We want to know v20. It is good to have a hunger for knowledge and be open to new ways of growing in our faith.

17:22-34 Paul's Second Recorded Sermon

The Greeks were unfamiliar with the Jewish culture and heritage so Paul changed his approach - he identified a local UNKNOWN GOD -

• God made and controls everything v24
• God gives all men life and breath and everything else v25
• from one man God made all nations and he determines the times set for them and the exact places where they should live v26
• God wants men to seek him, reach out for him and find him v27
• God is everywhere present – omnipresent - in God we live and move and have our being v28
• God commands all people to repent because a day of judgment is set and Jesus is appointed as judge v30,31
• proof of this is the fact that God raised Jesus from the dead v31.

The message concluded with a challenge for the hearers to respond to Jesus as Savior and Lord. Each person must face these truths eventually. We should always encourage people to make a decision to follow Jesus. Some sneered at the resurrection, as many do today   people tend to be antagonistic towards things they don't accept. A number believed and became followers. There is a wide range of human opinion about which we must make choices.

We can learn to use everyday issues, interests and objects to make opportunity to share the Gospel with others as Paul and Jesus did Jn 4:7; Lk 19:5.

17:23 TO AN UNKNOWN GOD

The Romans of the first century had a pantheon of gods. They also adopted the classical gods of the Greeks. Their gods were made in the image of man - they had human characteristics, physical features, emotions and attributes. Their Caesars could rise to the status of a god. It was possible for people to have any belief provided they annually bowed to an idol and professed Caesar as lord. This demand was to cause the martyrdom of many Christians who recognized Jesus only as Lord 17:7.

The Egyptians also adopted creatures and objects of nature as gods. All cultures throughout the generations have adopted gods in the image of man and nature to account for the innate sense of a greater being.

Yet despite this materialism, the Romans and many other people groups had a sense that there was more to existence than just a physical world. It was this God that the apostle Paul introduced to the Athenians.

This God made himself known through the Old Testament Gen 14:18-24; Ex 3:14 and was intimately revealed through Jesus by his exemplary life, self-sacrifice and resurrection reasonably attested by secular history 1:3 (ref p3).[2] Jesus declared he was the Son of God - it was for this claim that he was crucified Mt 26:63; Mk 14:61; Lk 22:70; Jn 19:7.

In the modern world many have rejected the concept of God. They use science and evolution as a reason for denying the Creator. Some have come to conclude that there is no need for God. There are many unknowns - what went before the big bang? - what was the source of the energy that produced matter and now fills and drives the universe? - what accounts for the fine tuning of the initial conditions and the many parameters and laws required to produce and sustain a unique world that is just right for human life? - what directed the progression of the inert atom to the pinnacle of the human intellect?

Believers see evidences of God's presence and purpose in the universe and in their personal experiences - they find no conflict between natural science and faith in God as revealed in the Bible. Even great thinkers of the natural sciences have struggled with this issue -

"It would be very difficult to explain why the universe should have begun in just this way, except as the act of a God who intended to create beings like us." - Hawking, cosmologist.[9]

"A common sense interpretation of the facts suggests that a super-intelligent has monkeyed with physics, as well as with chemistry and biology - the numbers - put this conclusion almost beyond question' - Hoyle, astronomer.[10]

"That man - his origins, his growth, his hopes, his loves and his beliefs - are destined to extinction - beneath the debris of a universe in ruin - only on the firm foundation of unyielding despair can the soul's salvation be safely built" - Russel atheist[11]

There is also the moral dilemma. Despite the best efforts of science human nature must still be constrained by laws of conduct. Corruption, conflict, deceit, domination, self-interest and desire for independence from authority continue.

The Ten Commandments given to Moses over 3,000 years ago are the foundation of western society but are continually being challenged by those who see truth as relative to personal opinion and consensus Ex 20:1-17.

The physical sciences cannot account for the spiritual realm. Science is defined as a systematic study of humans and the physical world based on reproducible observations, measurements and experiments.

The Bible reveals God as Spirit Jn 4:23,24. As such the physical human must come into a spiritual relationship in order to relate to the eternal God - *flesh gives birth to flesh but the Spirit gives birth to spirit Jn 3:3-8*. Beyond all is the mystery of the purpose of the universe and the individual destiny of mankind. The Bible reveals that those who reject its truths and deny its author will one day stand before an Unknown God.

18:1-8 **Corinth** There was not a significant response from the philosophers. Paul left Athens and moved west to Corinth, capital of the Roman province of Achaia since AD 44. There he met Aquila and Prisilla, believers who had been expelled from Rome and now assisted him. He worked with them as a tentmaker for a time, preaching in the synagogue on the Sabbath.

When Silas and Timothy arrived, Paul devoted himself totally to preaching to the Jews. They opposed him for claiming the deity of Jesus. So he turned to the Gentiles v6. To this point his main focus had been to give Jews the opportunity first to accept the Gospel due to his concern for them.

Many did believe and were baptized v8.

Jesus is the Christ (Messiah, the Anointed One) v5 - This is the title by which Paul referred to the Lord amongst the Jews. It acknowledges that Jesus is the foretold Messiah but also states the full deity of Jesus as the Son of God, co-equal and co-eternal with the Father 13:32-35; Ps 2:7; Is 9:6,7; Phil 2:5-11; Col 1:15-20. This is an essential and unique claim of the Bible.

The naturalist appeals to human reason as the only measure of knowledge. However in the realm of the Spirit there are truths that can only be understood by faith - *without controversy great is the mystery of godliness: God was manifest in the flesh, justified in the Spirit, seen of angels, preached unto the Gentiles, believed on in the world, received up into glory 1Tit 3:16;* Heb 11:1.

***18:9-18* Many Believed** Paul was encouraged by the Lord to keep on speaking so he stayed in Corinth teaching for one and a half years - meeting with further success v9-11. He also encountered persecution and was brought before the local proconsul Gallio AD 53 by the Jews, but the case was rejected v16.

While in Corinth, Paul received a good report from Timothy which led to the two Epistles to the Thessalonians 1Thes 3:6. The main theme was the return of Jesus and the need to remain faithful against persecution.

18:18-21 Paul eventually left Corinth and sailed to Ephesus, then on to Caesarea. Silas and Timothy remained behind to administer the churches.

***18:22,23* Third Visit to Jerusalem** From Caesarea Paul visited the church in Jerusalem again. There appears to have been no issues compared with his previous visit. He then returned to Antioch and ministered there for some time v23.

The Second Mission Journey had extended the church from Galatia and Asia Minor into Europe - Macedonia and Greece. The major issues of doctrine and practice within the early church were by now formally resolved.

THE THIRD MISSION JOURNEY AD 54 – 57 (18:23 to 21:16)

18:23 Paul set out alone to revisit **Galatia and Phrygia** strengthening the disciples. This was his main focus on this journey. He returned to all of the centres in Asia Minor, Macedonia and Greece he had visited on the second journey.

18:24-28* Apollos** a fervent teacher and preacher came to **Ephesus**. He was refined in his understanding of the Gospel by Aquila and Prisilla, who were already discipling in their home group v6. Apollos was taught by them and received the baptism of the Holy Spirit. He then went to teach in **Achaia** in **Greece** where he was a great help to the believers, ***proving from the Scriptures that Jesus was the Christ v28.

***19:1-7* Ephesus** Paul met twelve disciples of John. They had accepted Jesus as Messiah due to the teaching of John the Baptist - *Look, the Lamb of God, who takes away the sin of the world Jn 1:29.* Paul recognized that they lacked evidence of the Holy Spirit in their ministry and teaching. He instructed them and baptized them in the name of Jesus. He then laid hands on them and they received the baptism of the Holy Spirit. They then continued on with their teaching ministry.

These events indicate the large number of disciples who were circulating in ministry through the world by this time.

19: 8-20 **Ministry for two years** Paul taught and preached in the synagogue and then in a lecture hall. He remained there for two years v10. Miracles were performed, counterfeits were punished, the people were filled with fear and the name of the Lord Jesus was held in high honor v17. Many confessed and repented and the Word of the Lord spread widely and grew in power v20.

At Ephesus Paul received news of problems with the believers in Corinth - by visitors and a letter 1Cor 1:11; 7:1. He wrote the first Epistle to the Corinthians addressing fourteen issues at this time which he sent with Timothy 1Cor 4:17. He likely also made a short visit to Corinth to reinforce the letter before returning to Ephesus 1Cor 4:19; 2Cor 13:1-3.

19:21,22 **Recall to Jerusalem** Paul decided that he must go back to Jerusalem. He had a plan to go to Rome Rom 1:11-13. In fact he wanted to go all the way to Spain to preach the Gospel to the ends of the earth Rom 15:24. From this point Paul began to farewell the people in Asia – he felt he might not see them again. He decided to travel indirectly back through Macedonia and Achaia.

19:23-41 **Resistance to the Way** A riot occurred in Ephesus before Paul left which shows the antagonism nonbelievers have towards the Gospel of Jesus. Craftsmen stirred up a protest in defense of an idol because it impacted their trade. Many of the participants were not even aware of the reason for the riot v32. The conflict made the city too dangerous for Paul.

People of the Way - a title used by the disciples referring to the statement of Jesus - *I am the way the truth and the life. No one comes to the Father except through me Jn 14:6.*

20:1 **Macedonia** After a formal farewell Paul left Ephesus and travelled to Macedonia. He spent time in **Troas** where people responded to the message before returning to Macedonia 2Cor 2:12,13. He was still troubled about the situation in Corinth and their response to his correction. Titus arrived in Macedonia with a good report that encouraged Paul 2Cor 7:6,7,13. He then produced the second Epistle to the Corinthians which was delivered by Titus.

20:2-6 **Greece** Paul then stayed in Greece for three months, most of the time in Corinth. He had much to revise with them now that they had responded to his authority and teaching 2Cor 13:10. This was his third visit 2Cor 13:1,2. There he likely wrote the Epistle to the Romans in preparation for his planned visit Rom 15:23-25; 16:23.

20:3 Because of a threat on his life by the Jews in Jerusalem he returned to Macedonia rather than sail directly back to Syria. Now accompanied by others including Luke, they sailed for Troas.

20:7-12 **Troas** Back in Troas the disciples met on the *first day of the week* to break bread v7.

During the teaching a lad was brought back to life v10.

The Lord's Day v7 This was the common occurrence with the disciples from the beginning and confirms the significance of the Lord's Day and the practice of Communion with the believers.

There is no historical or Biblical record of the early Christians meeting on Saturday or 'keeping the Sabbath'. From the beginning the believers were not included in the Temple worship up to AD 70 or in the synagogues unless they conformed to the Jewish rituals. There was aggressive antagonism towards them.

Before the Jewish rebellion began in AD 66 the believers became separated from the Jews.

Paul went to the synagogues when he entered a new location seeking a sympathetic hearing for the Gospel but soon left the Jewish community and often the location due to persecution and riots 13:14,44,45; 17:1-5; 18:1-6.

The first believers met every day in the Temple courts 2:46. They celebrated breaking of bread together in their houses 2:46; 1Cor 11:20. On the first day of the week they came together to break bread 20:7; Jn 20:19,26; 1Cor 16:1,2.

It was the Lord's Day and celebrated the resurrection of the Lord Mk 16:2. The Lord's Supper was often celebrated at dawn or in the evening as slaves were required to work.

There were no Jewish customs, rules or laws placed on the believers by the Jerusalem Council in AD 49 15:23-29. John the apostle, recognised the Lord's Day around AD 90 Rev 1:10.

One man considers one day more sacred than another; another man considers every day alike. Each one should be fully convinced in his own mind Rom 14:4-8; Gal 3:23-26; 4:8-1; Col 2:13-17; Heb 8:6,7; Jas 2:1-12.

Jesus explained *the Sabbath was made for man, not man for the Sabbath Mk 2:22-28*; Mt 12:1-13; Lk 6:1-11; 14:1-6; Jn 5:1-18.

The Lord's Day fulfilled the benefits and function of the Sabbath, not under the old written code, but in the new way of the Spirit Rom 7:6. It is a remembrance of the Lord Lk 22:19.

Historical records show that the early church leaders were unanimous in teaching and keeping the first day of the week (Sunday) as the Lord's day -

• The Didache appeared around AD 90 with 'instructions of the disciples' about assembling on the Lord's Day.

• Ignatius, Bishop of Antioch AD 110 speaking of Jewish Christians wrote – "they have given up keeping the Sabbath and now order their lives by the Lord's Day instead"[12]

• Many other church writers referred to the keeping of the Lord's Day - Justin Martyr, Christian apologist AD 150; Clement of Alexandria AD 190; Tertullian of Carthage, North Africa AD 203; Origen of Alexandria AD 229; Eusebius, Bishop of Caesarea AD 300; Athanasius of Alexandria AD 345.

The Lord's Supper v7 The practice of Communion, 'breaking bread', was introduced at the last supper in the upper room when Jesus instituted the New Covenant. He took the bread and wine and gave it to his disciples to partake of it, as representing his body, broken on the cross for them and his blood, shed on the cross for them, with the words *do this in remembrance of me Lk 22:19,20*. This act symbolized the crucifixion which was about to take place as a sacrifice for the sins of all who would commit their lives to Jesus as Savior and Lord. Paul celebrated this simple act in line with the other disciples. It was called the 'Lord's Supper' and is the regular solemn practice of all believers throughout the world *for whenever you eat this bread and drink this cup, you proclaim the Lord's death until he comes 1Cor 11:23-26*.

The celebration on the Lord's Day included -

• assembling for worship, singing praise and prayer

• reading of the Word and teaching – many could not read and documents were few

• the 'breaking of bread' – the Lord's Supper - also called the 'Eucharist' (Greek, grateful thanksgiving) or holy communion

• the fellowship meal – love feast – sharing of a meal to demonstrate the common bond and to bless the poor 2:46

Acts of the Apostles

- Paul instructed the Corinthians in these matters 1Cor 11:17-34.

***20:13-21* The Gospel Confirmed** Paul's party sailed from Troas down the coast of Asia to Miletus where there was a farewell visit with elders who came from Ephesus v17,18.

Paul again emphasized the Gospel The basic principle of the Gospel is – *that they must turn to God in repentance and have faith in our Lord Jesus v21.*

***20:22-24* Total commitment** Paul had come to complete trust in Jesus in regard to every aspect of his life and ministry - *the life I live in the body, I live by faith in the Son of God, who loved me and gave himself for me Gal 2:20.* He expressed apprehension about his future but determined to go on – he was *compelled by the Spirit v22.* We must learn to recognize, encourage and respond to this compelling work of the Holy Spirit in our own lives 1Kin 19:11-13.

***20:25-38* Final Teaching** Paul encouraged the elders to follow his example by being good shepherds of the believers. He knew that wolves would attempt to distort the truth and draw people away from faith v28-31. He also encouraged hard work as it is more blessed to give than to receive v35 - this is the Protestant work ethic which has been so important in the advancement of western society and in the lives of those who apply it. He believed he would not see them again v25,38.

***20:32* The Word of God's Grace** v32 The Word, the expression of God, referred to the Old Testament Scriptures, the Books of the Torah - the Law and the Books of history, prophets and wisdom. It is regarded as permanent - *Your Word, O Lord, is eternal; it stands firm in the heavens Ps 119:89.* It was the foundation of faith, life and society Jos 1:8.

To the early believers the Word took in the teaching revealed by Jesus and his whole way of life Mt 4:4; Lk 24:44,45; Jn 1:1,14.

The Word now incorporates the New Testament – the Gospels, Book of Acts and the Epistles as fulfillment of the Old Testament.

While the reliability of the Bible is well attested (ref p2) confidence in the Scriptures is affirmed by the testimony of Jesus who quoted from most books of the Old Testament Mt 4:1-11; 5:17-38; 12:17; 19:3-4 and referred to the characters and places as real people and locations - Noah Mt 24:38; Jonah Mt 12:39; Sodom Mt 10:15; Moses Mt 8:4; David Mt 22:42-46; Solomon and Sheba Mt 12:42. He declared that not one stroke will disappear until all is accomplished Mt 5:17,18.

The Word of God is inspired – God-breathed - God breathed on the various authors inspiring them to write his will. It contains all we need for salvation and victorious, effective living 2Tim 3:15,16; 2Pet 1:20,21. God will breathe on you when you open it and seek to hear from him Heb 4:12,13.

- **I commit you to God and to the Word of his grace** v32 The believer grows primarily by application of the spiritual disciplines on a regular basis
- **It will build you up and give you an inheritance for eternal life** v32 - if you read God's Word, delight in it and meditate on it day and night Ps 1:2; 1Pet 1:23
- **Jesus is called the Word of God** because he the direct expression of God - *the radiance of God's glory and the exact representation of his being Heb 1:3*; Jn 1:1;14.

21:1-11 **The return to Jerusalem** From Miletus they sailed back to **Tyre** then to **Caesarea** and stayed with Philip, one of the seven deacons. In each place prophecy was made about Paul's impending imprisonment v11.

21:12-16 **He would not be dissuaded** Paul was proud of his Jewish heritage which he preserved to the end 22:2,3; 26:4-4; Rom 11:1; 2Cor 11:22. But beyond that he was a follower of Jesus – he considered all things as rubbish in comparison with gaining Christ Phil 3:4-11. So the thought of suffering further for Jesus was not a concern. *When he would not be dissuaded we gave up and said 'The Lord's will be done' v14.* It is necessary to be beyond persuasion if we are to achieve great things for the Lord.

They then stayed with Mnason, one of the early disciples v16.

ARREST IN JERUSALEM and CAESAREA AD 58 (21:17 to 26:32)

21:17-20 **Fourth Visit to Jerusalem** Paul's group went to Jerusalem and reported to James, head of the Council 15:13 and the elders and leaders of the church in Jerusalem. Peter and John were not mentioned, no doubt on ministry work (this visit was a decade after the previous council meeting).

Paul also presented the financial gifts given by the Gentile believers for the saints in the city Rom 15:23-29; 1Cor 16:1-4; 2Cor 8:1-7; 9:1-5. This was a major reason for the return to Jerusalem before the planned mission journey to Rome on the way to Spain 24:17.

Paul then reported on the work done among the Gentiles which brought praise from the elders v19.

21:20-26 **Conflict with the Jewish rituals** Paul was warned about the threats of the Jews. Many Jewish people had also believed the Gospel and become followers of Jesus. But they still insisted on strict adherence to the Jewish Law. They had false understanding of what Paul had been teaching about grace - he was not speaking against the customs but declaring that the observance of the ritual Law was not a condition of salvation v20,21. This attempt to retain Jewish customs in the new faith was resisted by the believers.[12]

Paul also had to contend with his old Pharisee colleagues in Jerusalem and some Jewish people who had come from Asia having caused trouble for him during his mission journeys.

At the request of the elders Paul joined in a Jewish rite to pacify the antagonists v24. This compromise proved to be of no avail.

21:27-40 **Paul's Arrest** Paul's presence in the Temple caused a major disturbance when he was recognized by the Jews from Asia. We must avoid fanatical confrontation if we are to promote the Gospel of peace. Paul was arrested for his own safety v33.

Paul was permitted to address the crowd making every opportunity to proclaim the Gospel.

22:1-21 **Paul's Third Recorded Sermon**

Paul showed his linguistic ability as well as his oratory skill -

• he presented his credentials as a Jew and explained how he had persecuted the believers v3-5

• he witnessed his direct encounter with Jesus in a vision v6-10

• he explained how God chose him to know his will, to see the Righteous One, Jesus, and to hear him speak v14.

• he then boldly described his commission from the Lord to present the Gospel to the Gentiles in distant places v21.

22:22 **The Response** Paul's reference to acceptance of the Gentiles caused another riot. This was the environment in which the universal message of faith in Jesus was to prosper.

22:23-30 **Paul's Roman Citizenship** Taken to the jail Paul was about to be flogged for disturbing the peace when he declared his Roman citizenship which granted him immunity from punishment without a trial v25. The Roman commander did not understand why the people were so incensed by Paul. He sent Paul to appear before the Sanhedrin, the highest Jewish Council because the charge against him related to Jewish Law and Custom v30.

23:1-10 Address to the Sanhedrin Paul's presentation to the Sanhedrin caused division and an uproar when he declared *I stand on trial because of my hope in the resurrection of the dead v6*. Sadducees did not believe in the resurrection while the Pharisees did. What joy to be able to place one's hope in the resurrection of the dead. The dispute became so violent that Paul's life was in danger and he was confined under arrest.

23:11-22 A death plot Paul was again encouraged by the Lord that he would testify in Rome v11. A plot to take Paul's life was exposed and reported to the prison commander.

23:23-35 Transfer to Caesarea As the matter involved Jewish Law and Paul was a Roman citizen the prison commander provided escort for Paul to Caesarea to be tried by Felix, Roman governor of Judea AD 52-60.

24:1-9 Trial before Felix Paul was brought before Felix. The charges against him were spurious indicating the rigid nature of their culture and claims v5-9. Paul was accused of being a ringleader of the Nazarene sect – a follower of Jesus! v5.

24:10-23 Paul's Fourth Recorded Sermon

Paul's defense was based on his good conduct and his belief in the resurrection from the dead -

• he denied the claim of stirring up a riot – he had done nothing against the law of the land v12

• he identified that the God who raised Jesus was the God of the Old Testament, the 'God of our fathers' v14

• he confessed to being a follower of the Way v14; Jn 14:6

• he confirmed his support for the Law and the Prophets v14

• he believed in *a resurrection of both the righteous and the wicked* as the Pharisees claimed to believe v15

• he strived to keep his conscience clear before God and man v16

• he came to Jerusalem with gifts for the poor v17

• his only crime and reason for trial could be his belief in the resurrection of the dead v21.

There was no verdict and Paul remained under guard v23.

24:24-27 Private audience Felix requested a private hearing. Paul *spoke about faith in Christ Jesus – on righteousness, self-control* *and the judgment to come v24.* No wonder the governor was afraid! He discussed the matter of judgment and resurrection with Paul many times v25,26. Paul spent the next two years in Caesarea at the governor's pleasure v27.

25:1-12 Trial before Festus The new governor Festus AD 60-62 reviewed Paul's case at the request of the Jews and chief priests who wanted him back in Jerusalem where they had more influence. Rather than face the murderous threat of the Jews Paul used his privileged status as a Roman citizen to appeal to be tried in Rome under Caesar. Festus was obliged to send Paul to Rome - *to Caesar you will go! v12.* This achieved Paul's objective!

The trials before these two governors confirm the date of Paul's confinement in Caesarea and Rome.

25:13-27 Further testimony Agrippa, puppet king of west Galilee AD 48-66 came to Caesarea and was asked by Festus to comment on Paul's case. It involved *a dead man named Jesus who Paul claimed was alive v19.* The issue was clear in the mind of the governor!

Agrippa and his retinue entered with the pomp and ceremony of the times v23. Festus was looking for a definite charge to accompany Paul to Rome v27.

26:1 Before Agrippa II This special hearing was for the benefit of Agrippa so Paul was given permission to speak.

26:2-23 Paul's Fifth Recorded Sermon
Paul gave his testimony - a great way to witness - with an appeal at the end.

• he respectfully acknowledged the position of Agrippa v2,3
• he declared his former role as a strict Pharisee v4-8
• he believed that the hope promised by God to 'our fathers' and expected by the Jewish people had now been received
• he explained that he had opposed and zealously persecuted the name of Jesus v9-11; 9:4
• through a vision he came to regard the one he had persecuted to be Jesus Christ the Lord and Messiah of the Scriptures v12-18
• he became a follower of Jesus and was commissioned to take the message of salvation to the Gentiles throughout the world v19,20
• he confirmed that what he now believed agreed with what Moses and the prophets had said - that the Christ would suffer and be the first to rise

from the dead with the assurance that all who believe in him will follow, both Jew and Gentile v23; Jn 11:25,26.

26:24-32 **Response** Festus, the governor could not understand the reality of Paul's experience and testimony - he considered Paul to be out of his mind v24,25.

Physical science sees the world objectively through the five senses. The humanist thinks in terms of human effort and achievement. The person of faith has come to encounter the spiritual realm which cannot be explained in physical and humanistic concepts Jn 4:24-26. The mind set on what human nature desires is in conflict with the mind set on what the Spirit of God desires Rom 8:5-8.

Agrippa would not be persuaded but found Paul to be without fault v30-32. As there were no further charges against Paul he could have been released had he not appealed to be heard before Caesar.

JOURNEY TO ROME AD 58 – 60 (27:1 to 28:31)

27:1-44 **Voyage to the Capital** Under military escort Paul together with Luke and friends sailed for Italy. They suffered severe weather and were ultimately shipwrecked. They were saved by miraculous intervention v23-26. They came ashore on Malta v44.

28:1-14 **Ministry on Malta** Kindness was shown by the local people. Miracles and healings occurred and the Gospel was preached.

After three months they sailed on to **Rome.**

28:15 **Paul In Rome** On arrival in Rome AD 60 Paul was greeted outside the city by believing brothers, many of whom were known to him. They would have received his Epistle to the Romans sent from Corinth AD 57. There did not seem to be an organised assembly – there were many house groups Rom 1:7; 16:5,10-12,14,15.

The Church in Rome The believers in Rome were not of Paul's making Rom 15:20. There were many paths by which the Gospel could have reached the city. The Jews had been expelled from Rome by Claudius AD 49 but had now returned.

There is no reference to Peter in Paul's Epistle to the Romans or during his meetings in Rome.

Mark spent time with Paul during his confinement in Rome as a valuable assistant together with Luke where they would have conferred on the content of their Gospel accounts Col 4:10,14; Phm 1:24.

28:16 **House detention** Paul was allowed to live in Rome under house arrest awaiting trial for two years which gave him the opportunity to preach the Gospel to all who came by v16.

28:17-23 **The Hope of Israel** Paul then called together the Jewish leaders in Rome and explained his calling and the reason for his arrest. The Jewish community had not received any information from Jerusalem about Paul and seemed unfamiliar with the Gospel v22,22. However they gave him a willing audience.

He had *done nothing against our people or against the customs of our ancestors v17*. He confirmed that he, along with all Jewish people looked forward to the Messiah, the **'Hope of Israel'** as foretold by the prophets in the Old Testament Scriptures v20. He proclaimed that Jesus was the one who fulfilled this role – *he tried to convince them about Jesus from the Law of Moses and from the Prophets v23; 9:22.*

28:23 **Convincing them about Jesus** While the Book of Acts draws attention to the actions of the believers - Peter, Paul, Barnabas and the many disciples it is important to recognize that the primary focus of the Book and their message is the Person of Jesus. He is the central theme of all their teaching, preaching and endeavors. They lived to proclaim the Gospel - that Jesus died and rose again to bring eternal life to those who believe 1Cor 15:3,4.

This is the fact about which we must each make a decision -

And this is the testimony: God has given us eternal life,
and this life is in his Son. He who has the Son has life;
he who does not have the Son of God does not have life Jn 5:11,12

28:24-29 **Salvation is a matter of choice** After declaring the Gospel, the good news about Jesus to the Jewish leaders there was a mixed response – some of the Jews believed the message but others would not. This outcome was predicted by the prophets Is 6:9,10.

Eternal life through faith in Jesus is still a matter of choice. Paul confirmed that God's salvation was available not only to the Jews but to the Gentiles as well v28.

28:30,31 **Preaching the Gospel in Rome** For the next two years while under house arrest in the centre of the known world Paul *boldly and*

without hindrance - preached the kingdom of God and taught about Jesus Christ.
He also wrote a number of letters to the churches – the 'prison epistles'! (ref p 78).

End of the Book of Acts The narrative ends suddenly with Paul still in Rome under house arrest and with the Gospel expanding. Later events are not mentioned. This contrasts with the continuity and detail of Luke's Gospel and Book of Acts indicating that the events were documented concurrently with the activities leading up to the early AD 60's.

28:31 The Unique Gospel of the Kingdom of God
Some see all gods as the same; some deny or reject the concept of god altogether. Some say all paths lead to the same destination. There are many beliefs and philosophies that claim the attention of people.
The Bible has a right and a necessity to claim uniqueness -
• **Unique God** - Eternal Spirit, Creator of the universe, absolute good, perfect love - who progressively revealed himself Gen 2:4; Ex 3:14 - a personal being who chose to intervene in world affairs by sending his Son to redeem mankind
• **Unique Savior** - who came from God - an historical figure, of exemplary life and teaching - crucified without fault as a sacrifice for sin - by his resurrection from the dead was proved to be the Savior of all who put their trust in him – the only One who offers salvation and eternal life to the believer
• **Unique Bible** - containing the only continuing record of God's relationship with mankind over two millennia until the way of salvation for mankind was secured (from pre 2000 BC).

Conclusion - Within thirty years of the resurrection and ascension the message of Jesus Christ as Savior and Lord spread from a remote corner of the world to impact people of all nations Col 1:23. This was in response to the command of Jesus to go into the entire world Mt 28:18-20. The Gospel continues to bless and expand today.

Journeys Inferred in the Epistles -
There were other possible events and journeys in the life of Paul
- Paul was released from house arrest in Rome after 2 years AD 62. There was no charge pursued against him possibly because of the fear of the Jewish leaders to go to Rome 18:2
- He returned to Ephesus where he had left Timothy 1Tim 1:3
- More time was spent in Macedonia 1Tim 1:3
- He was again in Crete where he had left Titus Tit 1:5
- He spent a winter in Nicopolis Tit 3:12
- Arrangements were made for a visit to Colosse Phm 1:22
- There was a plan to go to Spain Rom 15:24,25
- Paul was arrested and imprisoned in Rome again 2Tim 4:6-18
- He is believed to have been martyred (beheaded, as a Roman citizen) AD 67 under the persecution of Roman Emperor Nero AD 54-68.

Future events in the early Church –

Little is known of the activities of the other apostles Mk 3:13-19 apart from tradition. We can be thankful for the methodical writings of Luke, companion of Paul and the other Gospel writers that have been preserved to provide us with the basic necessities of the first century period.

Mark went to Cyprus with Barnabas in AD 50 and was next reported to be ministering in Alexandria.[12] After the Jerusalem Council in AD 50 Peter left Jerusalem and ministered in central and north Asia Minor and may have led the church in Antioch for a time 1Pet 1:1. He was accompanied by Mark as his assistant and interpreter. They are reported to be in Rome in the late AD 50's where Mark prepared his Gospel based on Peter's preaching and teaching.[12]

Peter appears to be absent from Rome during Paul's detention AD 60-62. Mark assisted Paul during this period, together with Luke Col 4:10,14; Phm 1:24.

After Paul's release he went on further mission work (ref p64). He was rearrested and martyred in Rome around AD 67 under Nero.

Peter is also believed to have be in Rome with Mark AD 62-67 where he wrote his first Epistle 1Pet 5:13. Peter was arrested and martyred in Rome by crucifixion under Nero 2Pet 1:13,14.[12]

At the time of Paul's death Judea was in revolt against the Romans due to excessive taxes and confiscation of Temple funds (from AD 66). In AD 70 after a prolonged siege Titus destroyed the city of Jerusalem and the Temple as Jesus had predicted Mt 24:1,2 bringing an end to the Levitical Sacrificial System. The Sanhedrin and high priesthood were abolished and Jewish worship only continued through the synagogues which had been established in the Babylonian exile period.

Further uprisings resulted in Emperor Hadrian expelling the Jews from Jerusalem and building a Roman city Aelia Capitolina in its place AD 135 in an attempt to eradicate the Jewish faith.

For 1,900 years the Jewish people were persecuted around the world until May 14, 1948 when the Jewish people became a 'nation in a day' and were re-established in their homeland Is 66:8; Jer 16:14,15.

They are now at the centre of the world stage and will be prominent in the end time Zec 12:1-5; Rom 11:26-32.

Acts of the Apostles

Prominent Rulers of the First Century

Roman Emperors
The main emperors of the first century -

Octavian Augustus	29 BC-AD14	at the birth of Jesus
Tiberius	AD 14-37	throughout the ministry of Jesus
Caligula	AD 37-41	during the ministry of Peter, Barnabas and Paul
Claudius	AD 41-54	Paul and Barnabas took famine relieve
Nero	AD 54-68	blamed Christians for burning Rome AD 64
Vespasian	AD 69-79	besieged Jerusalem AD 66
Titus	AD 79-81	destroyed Jerusalem and the Temple AD 70
Domitian	AD 81-96	persecuted Christians - possibly Paul and Peter
Trajan	AD 98-117	subdued Christians throughout the Empire
Hadrian	AD 117-135	expelled all Jews and rebuilt Jerusalem as the Roman city Aelia Capitolina

Local Rulers of Judea (Herodians)
A number of members of Herod's family ruled in various localities -

Herod the Great	King of Judea	37-4 BC	Mt 2:1-22
Herod Antipas	Tetrarch of Galilee	4 BC-AD 39	Mt 14:1-10
Herod Agrippa I	King of Judea	AD 41-44	Acts 12:1-25
Herod Agrippa II	King, north Galilee	AD 48-66	Acts 25:1 to 26:3

Roman Procurators (Governors) of Judea
Augustus placed Roman governors over Judea from AD 4. There were many governors in this period who were mostly ineffective.
The key ones were -

Pontius Pilate	AD 26-36	Jn 18:18 to 19:22	crucified Jesus
Antonius Felix	AD 52-60	Acts 24:1-27	presided over Paul's trial
Porcius Festus	AD 60-62	Acts 25:1 to 26:32	presided over Paul's trial
Gessius Florus	AD 63-66	Time of the fall of Jerusalem	

Statements of Belief

The Gospels and the Epistles were not prepared as theological statements. The Gospels are primarily historical records of the life and teaching of Jesus. There were written documents of the Acts of Jesus - used in Mark's Gospel. Matthew used the Sayings and Teachings of Jesus. Luke confirmed that by the time he wrote his Gospel in the early AD 60's there were many accounts drawn up of the events surrounding the life, death and resurrection of Jesus - *the things that have been fulfilled among us, just as they were handed down to us by those who from the first were eyewitnesses Lk 1:1,2*

The Epistles were prepared as letters to the believers at various locations addressing relevant issues of the time.

As the church grew and multiplied through the known world of the time it was necessary to develop and document formal doctrine based on the beliefs of the apostles as set out in the Gospel message and the New Testament documents. This was undertaken by meetings of the church leaders at various cities and over time. The locations of these councils were all in northwest Asia Minor which shows the centre of activity of the church in the second and third centuries.

A number of heresies arose toward the end of the first and in the second centuries. Councils were called to clarify the teaching of the church.

Six General Councils are recognized as being universal with all areas of the early church being represented - [13]

Nicaea AD 325 - to define the Trinity in more detail.

Constantinople 1 AD 381 – to confirm the deity of the Holy Spirit.

Ephesus AD 431 – to confirm the Unity of Person of Jesus.

Chalcedon AD 451 – to clarify the distinction of Natures in the incarnation of Jesus.

Other Councils were held at Constantinople II, AD 553 and Constantinople III, AD 680.

The statements of belief resulting from these Councils are –

• The Apostles Creed – outlines the basic beliefs and teaching of the first Apostles

• The Nicene Creed – defines more clearly the eternal Sonship of Jesus

• The Athanasian Creed – defines more clearly the deity of each Person of the Trinity within the Godhead

• The Chalcedon Creed – further defines the two natures of Jesus as regards his Godhead and his Manhood – truly God and truly man.

Since the Reformation a number of valuable statements have been formulated within the denominations to classify teaching and belief. However these four major Creeds still represent the foundation truths of the Christian Church as taught by the Apostles and contained in the Word of God. They contain all that is required for salvation and effective service 2Tim 3:15-17.

The earliest major creed, developed from the earlier documents appeared around AD 215 as the Apostles Creed which formed the basis for later Creeds.[14]

The Apostles Creed

I believe in God, the Father, Almighty;
Maker of heaven and earth:
And in Jesus Christ his only Son our Lord,
Who was conceived by the Holy Spirit;
Born of the Virgin Mary,
Suffered under Pontius Pilate,
Was crucified, dead and buried,
He descended into hell;
The third day He rose again from the dead,
He ascended into heaven
And is seated at the right hand of God the Father Almighty;
From there he will come to judge the living and the dead.
I believe in the Holy Spirit;
The Holy Universal Church;
The communion of saints;
The forgiveness of sins;
The resurrection of the body;
And the life everlasting.

The Christian Worldview

The basic truths of the Christian Faith were revealed by Jesus and proclaimed by the first disciples as recorded in the New Testament. They are built on the Old Testament and seen as fulfilment of the many prophecies.

They are documented in the major statement of belief known as the Apostles Creed which is a development of the baptismal command of Jesus – *Therefore go and make disciple of all nations baptizing them in the name of the Father and of the Son and of the Holy Spirit Mt 28:19.* It contains the preaching messages of the Book of Acts and the teaching of the Epistles of Peter and Paul 1Pet 1:3-5; 1Cor 15:3-5 and was used in the baptismal service.

1. I believe in God, the Father, Almighty, maker of heaven and earth

• Personal acknowledgment of God – the Bible recognizes the existence of one eternal, self-existing God, who is Spirit Is 57:15; Jn 4:24
• Almighty – God in the Old Testament is revealed as Almighty, holy and to be worshipped and obeyed Gen 17:1; Is 6:1-3
• Maker of heaven and earth – all things belong to God, by right of creation, sustenance and redemption – this is declared from the beginning Gen 1:1; Is 42:5; Acts 17:24-28
• Father – Jesus revealed that God is also personal and desires a relationship with mankind as Father with a child Jn 1:12,13; 2Cor1:3; 1Pet 1:23; 1Jn 3:1
• Trinity – Jesus declared himself to be the Son of God. He predicted the coming of the Person of the Holy Spirit to dwell in the hearts of all believers 2Cor 13:14. The disciples proclaimed the Triune nature of the Godhead - *God has raised this Jesus to life – exalted to the right hand of God – he has received from the Father the promised Holy Spirit and has poured out what you now see and hear 2:33.*

2. And in Jesus Christ his only Son our Lord

• Lord Jesus Christ – From the ascension, the disciples recognized Jesus as Christ (Messiah, the Anointed One) and Lord - *God hath made this Jesus, whom you crucified, both Lord and Christ 2:36; Who believed in the Lord Jesus Christ 11:17; He taught about the Lord Jesus Christ 28:31; Lk 2:11; Jn 13:13; Rom 1:4; 14:9*

- God's only Son – Jesus has the unique position as the only begotten Son of God from eternity Mt 11:27; Heb 1:1-3. This was confirmed at the Baptism and the Transfiguration Mt 3:17; 17:5; Rom 1:4

3. Who was conceived by the Holy Spirit, Born of the Virgin Mary

- The incarnation (clothed with flesh) – It was necessary for the eternal Son of God to become human in the flesh to be a sinless sacrifice - *What is conceived in her is from the Holy Spirit Mt 1:20-23; The virgin will be with child and will give birth to a son and they shall call him Immanuel, 'God with us' Mt 1:23; The Word became flesh Jn 1:14.*
- Jesus is truly God and truly Man – two natures in one Person. Evidence is seen in the sinless and miraculous life of Jesus.
- While Jesus emptied himself of his deity, God the Father still presided and God the Holy Spirit still ministered Mt 3:16,17; 4:1; Phil 2:5-8.
- The incarnation - Spirit taking on flesh, confirms the eternal life of the believer, born again of the Spirit Jn 1:12,13; 3:6.

4. Suffered under Pontius Pilate, was crucified, dead and buried, He descended into hell

- The historicity of Jesus is noted under Pontius Pilate AD 26-36 - *The God of our fathers has glorified his servant Jesus. You handed him over to be killed and disowned him before Pilate, though he had decided to let him go 3:13.*
- Jesus had to die to remove the offense of sin before God Gal 4:4 - *For Christ died for sins once for all, the righteous for the unrighteous, to bring you to God 1Pet 3:18.* The fact of the physical death was confirmed by crucifixion and the death blow of a centurion. He was buried in the tomb of a reputable supporter.
- He descended into hell - hell in the Creed refers to the 'place of departed' awaiting judgment (Hades) Lk 16:22,23. This was necessary to confirm the reality of the manhood of Jesus - *But God raised him from the dead, freeing him from the agony of death, because it was impossible for death to keep its hold on him 2:24-28.*

5. The third day He rose again from the dead, He ascended into heaven

- The resurrection on the third day confirms the claims of Jesus to be the Son of God, to forgive sins and to give eternal life - *This Jesus hath*

*God raised up, whereof we all are witnesses 2:32; God raised him from
the dead on the third day and caused him to be seen 10:42; declared with
power to be the son of God by his resurrection from the dead Rom 1:2-4;
4:23-25*
• He ascended to heaven – the ascension vindicated the claims of Jesus
that he came from God and will return to gather the believers - *He was
taken up before their very eyes – will come back in the same way as you
have seen him go into heaven 1:9-11; He must remain in heaven until the
time comes for God to restore everything 3:2; He sat down at the right
hand of the Majesty in heaven Heb 1:3.*

6. And is seated at the right hand of God the Father Almighty
• The fullness of the deity of Jesus is restated – *the glory I had with you
before the world began Jn 17:5;*
• At the right hand of God - *God has raised this Jesus to life and –
exalted to the right hand of God 2:32,32; Phil 2:9-11; Heb 1:3*

7. From there he will come to judge the living and the dead
• He will come again to judge mankind - *He may send the Christ
3:20,21; He is the one whom God appointed as judge of the living and
the dead 10:42; He set a day when he will judge the world with justice
by the man he has appointed 17.31; Jn 5:22; Rom 14:10,12*
• There will be two outcomes based on the Lamb's Book of Life and the
books of deeds Rev 20:11-15.

8. I believe in the Holy Spirit
• The Holy Spirit impacted the first disciple, just as Jesus had told them.
He would be in them, teach them and empower them - *We are witness –
and so is the Holy Spirit whom God has given to those who obey him 5:32;
God has raised this Jesus to life – exalted to the right hand of God – he
has received from the Father the promised Holy Spirit and has poured
out what you now see and hear 2:33.*
• Those who commit to Jesus as Savior and Lord receive eternal life
and the Holy Spirit Acts 5:32.

9. The Holy Universal Church, The communion of saints
• The universal church (assembly). After Pentecost believers devoted
themselves to the apostles teaching 2:42-47. They met together regularly

and quickly resolved issues based on the teaching of Jesus and the Scriptures 5:11-16; 15:6,19,22,23.

• They were united in truth and message with the desire to spread the Good News of salvation through Jesus and the kingdom of God 5:19-21; 8:4; Mt 16:18; 28:18-20. They taught unity Eph 4:1-6

• The believer becomes a member of the 'body of Christ', independent of tribe, language, people, nation and denomination – *now your are the body of Christ 1Cor 12:12,13,27;* Rev 5:9

• All believers are united with those who went before – the company of heaven – *the great cloud of witness Heb 12:1; the assembly of the first born; the spirits of righteous men made perfect Heb 12:12-24.*

• We need the fellowship of other believers to encourage one another and work together Heb 10:23-25.

10. The forgiveness of sins

• Because mankind transgressed the holy nature of God, relationship was broken Gen 3:22; Rom 3:10-23; 6:23

• Forgiveness – Jesus came to give his life as a perfect sacrifice so that the offense of sin could be removed and those who accept him as Savior and Lord may have their sins forgiven - *He might give repentance and forgiveness of sins Acts 5:31; Through Jesus the forgiveness of sins is proclaimed to you Acts 13:38; So that they may receive forgiveness of sins Acts 26:18; Mt 1:21; Rom 4:24,25*

11. The resurrection of the body

• The resurrection of Jesus confirms the bodily resurrection of all mankind - *My hope in the resurrection of the dead 23:6; that there will be a resurrection of both the righteous and the wicked 24:15; Rom 8:11.*

• This truth provides eternal expectation for the believer compared with the materialistic view of oblivion *1Thes 4:14-17; Tit 2:13.*

12. And the life everlasting

• Eternal life - Jesus provides eternal life through faith and belief in him - *All who were appointed for eternal life believed 13:47,48; Tit 1:2; 3:7.*

• As the eternal Son of God took on physical life through the operation of the Holy Spirit so the one who believes in Jesus as Savior and Lord is born again and receives eternal life through the same Holy Spirit Lk 1:35; Jn 1:12.

The Historicity of Jesus

There have been numerous attempts to dispute, deny and explain away the life of Jesus – more so than any other person mentioned in history. This is understandable because of the statements Jesus made about himself and the claims he made on the life of the individual in all generations. The fact of the life, death and resurrection of Jesus is undeniable from the Bible record, from secular history and from the experience of the believer.

Some records of secular writers – these records from the first century put the reality of Jesus Christ as a person of history beyond doubt[2,3] -
Flavius Josephus – Jewish historian, scholar, defector to Rome AD 37-100 – writing around AD 90 in 'Antiquities of the Jews' recorded -
"There was about this time Jesus, a wise man, if it be lawful to call him a man, for he was a doer of wonderful works, a teacher of such men as receive the truth with pleasure. He drew over to him both many of the Jews and many of the Gentiles. He was the Christ and when Pilate, at the suggestion of the principal men among us, had condemned him to the cross, those that loved him at first did not forsake him: for he appeared to them alive again the third day; as the divine prophets had foretold these and ten thousand other wonderful things concerning him. The tribe of Christians so named from him are not extinct at this day."[2,3]
"John, surnamed the Baptist, for Herod had killed him – though he was a good man who bade – the people to come together for baptism."[2]
"Also the high priest Ananus – assembled a council of judges and brought before it the brother of Jesus the so-called Christ, whose name was James, together with some others and having accused them as law breakers, he delivered them over to be stoned."[2,3]
Tacitus – Roman senator and historian AD 56-117 – writing in AD 112 - in 'Annals' recorded - after the burning of Rome in AD 64 - "Nero - falsely charged with the guilt and punished with the most exquisite torture the persons commonly called Christians - Christus, the founder of the name was put to death by Pontius Pilate, procurator of Judes in the reign of Tiberius."[3]
Mara Bar-Serapion – Roman Stoic philosopher – sometime after AD 73 – wrote of the consequence of the Jews executing their wise King (Jesus) – their kingdom was abolished![2]

Suetonius – Roman historian under Hadrian AD 120 – writing about the period AD 64 – "As the Jews were making constant disturbances at the instigation of Chrestus (Christ) he expelled them from Rome."[3] Acts 18:2.

Pliny – governor of Bithynia in Asia Minor - writing to Emperor Trajan AD112 – about how to deal with Christians who refused to worship the Emperor – "the whole of their guilt – was that they were in the habit of meeting on a certain fixed day before it was light when they sang in alternate verse of hymn to Christ as God and bound themselves to a solemn oath (to good conduct)."[2,3]

Lucian Greek satirist and teacher – AD 115 mocked Christians about Jesus – "the man who was crucified in Palestine because he introduced this new cult into the world."[3]

Some records of early Christian writers – there are many documents of Christian leaders from the first and second centuries who wrote in the normal course of their duties[12,14] -

Didache - Instructions of the disciples about assembling on the Lord's Day AD 90

Clement, Bishop of Rome AD 30–97 - Epistle to Corinth

Ignatius, Bishop of Antioch AD 50–115 – Epistle to Magnesia

Papias, Bishop of Hierapolis AD 61-113 – Expositions

Polycarp, Bishop of Smyrna AD 69–156 – Epistle to Philippi

Irenaeus, Bishop of Lyons AD 90-180

Justin Martyr, philosopher, apologist AD 100–133.

Conclusion - The facts relating to the existence of Jesus are not the decisive issue. It is ultimately a matter of 'you believe or you do not!' This has been the experience of those who have chosen to believe and those who choose to deny – it is a personal decision. Intellectual ascent will not produce saving faith.

It is only by an act of faith in Jesus Christ – believing that he is the Son of God and the Saviour of all those who put their trust in him, that one can attain to eternal life.

For since in the wisdom of God the world through its wisdom did not know him, God was pleased through the foolishness of what was preached to save those who believe.

Jews demand miraculous signs and Greeks look for wisdom, but we preach Christ crucified: a stumbling block to Jews and foolishness to

Gentiles, but to those whom God has called, both Jews and Greeks, Christ, the power of God and the wisdom of God.
For the foolishness of God is wiser than man's wisdom and the weakness of God is stronger than man's strength 1Cor 1:21-25.

Chronology of Acts

		reference	date AD
Birth of the Church		1:1 to 2:47	30
	Ascension	1:1-11	
	Pentecost	2:1-13	
	Peter's First Sermon	2:14-41	
	The First Community - Characteristics	2:42-47	
Early Church in Jerusalem		3:1 to 7:60	31
	Healing a Cripple	3:1-26	
	Early Persecution	4:1-37	31
	Individual Commitment - Barnabas	4:32-37	
	Church Growth	5:1-16	
	Further Persecution	5:17-42	
Martyrdom of Stephen		6:1 to 7:60	33
	Conflict in the Church - Deacons Appointed	6:1-7	
	Stephen's Ministry & Death	6:8 to 7:60	
The Church Scattered		8:1 to 9:31	33
	Philip in Samaria	8:4-13	
	Peter & John in Samaria	8:14-25	
	Philip & the Ethiopian	8:26-40	
Conversion of Saul		9:1-31	33
	Damascus Road	9:1-19	
	Early Ministry of Saul	9:20-31	
The Gospel Received by the Gentiles		9:32 to 11:18	40
Conversion of Cornelius		10:1 to 11:18	
	Peter's Vision	10:1-23	
	Cornelius' Conversion	10:24-48	
	Peter explains his Actions	11:1-18	
The Gentile Church in Antioch		11:19-30	42
	Barnabas & Saul in Antioch	11:25-26	44
	Barnabas & Saul Visit Jerusalem	11:27-30	45
Persecution Continued		12:1-25	45
	James' Martydom	12:1-2	44
	Peter in Prison & Released	12:3-25	44

	reference	date AD
First Mission Journey	13:1 to 14:28	46 - 49
Cyprus & Galatia (Antioch, Iconium, Lystra & Derbe) - *Letter to Galatians*		
Jerusalem Council - Avoid Jewish Ceremmonial Law	15:1-35	50
Second Mission Journey	15:36 to 18:22	50 - 53
Galatia (Derbe, Lystra, Iconium & Antioch)		
Asia, Macedonia (Philippi, Thessalonica & Berea)		
Greece (Athens & Corinth) & Ephesus - *Letters to Thessalonians 1,2*		
Jerusalem Visit	18:22	
Third Mission Journey	18:23 to 21:16	54 - 58
Cilicia, Galatia, Asia, Macedonia & Greece		
Ephesus - *Letters to Rome & Corinthians 1,2*	19:1-41	
Farewells & Return to Jerusalem	20:1 to 21:16	
Paul in Jerusalem & Caesarea	21:16 - 26:32	58
Arrested - Before the Sanhedrin	21:17 to 23:22	
On Trial at Caesarea - Under Felix & Fesus	23:22 to 26:32	58 - 60
Paul's Journey to Rome	27:1 to 28:14	60
Under House Arrest in Rome	28:15-31	60
Letters to Ephesus, Colasse, Philippi, Philemon		
Letters to Timothy 1,2 & Titus		
Journeys Inferred in the Epistles		
Release from House Arrest in Rome	Rom 18:2	62
Visit to Ephesus - left Timothy	1Tim 1:3	
Visit to Macedonia	1Tim 1:3	
Visit to Crete - left Titus	Tit 1:5	
Visit to Nicopolis	Tit 3:12	
Visit to Colosse	Phile 22	
Possible Journey to Spain	Rom 15:24,25	
Under Arrest again in Rome		
Paul's Martydom - under Nero's presecution		67

Chronology of Acts

Outline of the Epistles

Epistles of Paul

	Epistle	date	from	theme
First Mission Journey				
	Galatians	AD 49	Antioch	Freedom from the Law through faith in Christ Jesus.
Second Mission Journey				
	1 Thessalonians	AD 51	Corinth	Holiness of living. Christ's return.
	2 Thessalonians	AD 51	Corinth	The Day of the Lord's return.
Third Mission Journey				
	1 Corinthians	AD 55	Ephesus	Instruction in daily living & spiritual gifts
	2 Corinthians	AD 56	Macedonia	Guidelines in discipleship
	Romans	AD 57	Corinth	God's gift of righteousness by faith in Christ alone
Prison Epistles				
	Ephesians	AD 60	Rome	New life in Christ. Spiritual warfare
	Philippians	AD 60	Rome	The joy of living for Christ.
	Colossians	AD 60	Rome	The supremacy of Christ & the Gospel
	Philemon	AD 60	Rome	Forgiveness.
Further Journeys & Prison				
	1 Timothy	AD 63	Macedonia	Leadership Manual
	Titus	AD 63	Macedonia	Conduct for Christian Living
	2 Timothy	AD 66	Rome	Endurance in pastoral ministry

General Epistles

Epistle	date	from	theme
Hebrews	AD 65	unknown	The Gospel of Jesus Christ is superior to the Old Covenant in all respects
James	AD 48	Jerusalem	Genuine faith produces action
1 Peter	AD 65	Rome	The glory of the believer's inheritance
2 Peter	AD 65	Rome	Warning against false teaching.
1 John	AD 90	Patmos	Deity of Jesus & assurance of salvation
2 John	AD 90	Patmos	Continue in love as we follow Jesus.
3 John	AD 90	Patmos	Be faithful in leadership.
Jude	unknown	Jerusalem	Beware of false teachers.
Revelation	AD 90	Patmos	Sovereignty of God & return of Jesus

The Acts of the Holy Spirit – in the Book of Acts

Introduction – It is useful to review the Book of Acts to identify the predominant influence and direction of the Holy Spirit in the work of the church.

1:2 Jesus gave instruction through the HOLY SPIRIT.

1:5 He told the disciples - *do not leave Jerusalem, but wait for the gift my Father promised – you will be baptized with the HOLY SPIRIT.*

1:8 He told them – *you will receive power when the HOLY SPIRIT comes on you and you will be my witnesses in Jerusalem - and to the ends of the earth.*

1:14 They joined together constantly in prayer, waiting as Jesus commanded.

1:16 They recognized the work of the HOLY SPIRIT in David.

1:24 They sought God's guidance through prayer in selecting Matthias.

2:1,2 At Pentecost, after 10 days of waiting together, obedient to what they had been told the promise came. They were all filled with the HOLY SPIRIT and began to witness, speaking in other tongues!

2:14 Peter stood up and preached with great boldness and ability.

2:17 Peter recognized that this was what God had promised Joel 2:28-32.

2:34 This was what Jesus had promised   what he had received from the Father and poured out Jn 16:7.

2:38 They received direction, new tongues, signs, power, words to speak, boldness, witnessing – 3,000 were added. This was the Birth of the Church.

4:8 Peter was arrested. Filled again with the HOLY SPIRIT he witnessed.

4:25 The people met and all prayed to speak the Word with great boldness – the place was shaken and they were all filled (again) with the HOLY SPIRIT and spoke the Word of God boldly – they witnessed.

5:3 The HOLY SPIRIT advised Peter of deception.

5:12 The apostles performed many miraculous signs and wonders – all who came were healed! The people were filled with awe.

5:17 The apostles were arrested and an angel released them. Arrested again, they were flogged and continued to witness.

5:28 **Jerusalem** was filled with the name of Jesus.

5:32 The HOLY SPIRIT is given by God to those who obey him.

5:41 They rejoiced at suffering for the name of Jesus and continued to proclaim the good news.

6:3 They identified the filling of the SPIRIT as a criterion for service.

6:5 Stephen was full of the HOLY SPIRIT. Appointed to serve great wonders and miraculous signs were done. He spoke boldly – witnessing.

7:55 Stephen was persecuted, but filled again with the HOLY SPIRIT, he accepted martyrdom.

8:1 As a result of Stephen's death persecution broke out – all except the apostles were scattered through **Judea and Samaria**.

8:4 Philip evangelized in Samaria and performed miraculous signs.

8:17 New believers received the HOLY SPIRIT when baptized.

8:26 An angel called Philip to go to Gaza, on a desert road. He obeyed.

8:29 The SPIRIT led him to an **Ethiopian** who was converted.

8:39 The SPIRIT of the Lord took Philip to his next assignment in **Caesarea**.

9:5 The SPIRIT of Jesus appeared to Saul and blinded him.

9:10-16 The Lord appeared to Ananias in a vision and told him to go to Saul – *This man is my chosen instrument to carry my name before the Gentiles - I will show him how much he must suffer for my name v15,16.*

9:17 Saul was filled with the HOLY SPIRIT.

9:31 The HOLY SPIRIT encouraged the believers in the Church in **Judea, Galilee, Samaria**.

10:1-10 An angel appeared to **Cornelius** to send for Peter who had a vision three times. The HOLY SPIRIT told him to go to **Caesarea**.

10:44,45 While Peter was speaking the HOLY SPIRIT came on all those Gentiles who heard. The Jews were astonished that the gift of the HOLY SPIRIT was poured out on the Gentiles.

11:16-18 Peter explained Cornelius was baptized with the HOLY SPIRIT. They concluded *God has granted even the Gentiles repentance unto life v18.*

11:19-21 Those who were scattered by persecution went as far as **Cyprus and Antioch** witnessing. A great number of people believed and turned to the Lord.

11:24-26 Barnabas, full of the HOLY SPIRIT brought Saul from Tarsus to assist in discipling and teaching at Antioch.

12:5 Peter was put in prison. The people prayed - an angel released him.

12:24 Despite persecution the Word of God continued to increase and spread.

13:1-3 Barnabas and Saul As the prophets and teachers were worshipping and fasting, the HOLY SPIRIT told them – *set apart for me Barnabas and Saul for the work to which I have called them.*

13:4 **THE FIRST MISSION JOURNEY** Barnabas and Saul were sent on their way by the HOLY SPIRIT to **Cyprus and Galatia**.

13:9 The HOLY SPIRIT filled Saul (Paul). A sorcerer was blinded and the local proconsul was converted.

13:48-52 Many Gentiles believed and the disciples were filled with joy and the HOLY SPIRIT.

14:23 Churches were established among the Gentiles. Elders were appointed with prayer and fasting.

15:8 The apostles and the whole Church at Jerusalem accepted the report of Paul and Barnabas that God had given the HOLY SPIRIT to the Gentiles.

15:28 Instruction to the Gentile Church was given through the HOLY SPIRIT.

15:36 **THE SECOND MISSION JOURNEY** Barnabas and Paul disagreed on the next step. They went different ways. Paul and Silas headed for Asia.

16:6-9 They were kept by the HOLY SPIRIT from preaching in Asia v6! They were prevented by the SPIRIT of Jesus from entering northern Asia v7! A vision took them to **Macedonia** and **Europe**. Their vision was not big enough!

16:25 In prison Paul and Silas prayed and sung hymns – the jailer was converted.

18:9 At Corinth the Lord reassured Paul in a vision.

19:6 **THE THIRD MISSION JOURNEY** At Ephesus some disciples were baptized in the HOLY SPIRIT.

20 :22 Paul was compelled by the SPIRIT to return to Jerusalem.

21:10 The HOLY SPIRIT warned Paul again of his fate in Jerusalem.

28:25 Paul recognized the HOLY SPIRIT spoke through Isaiah.

What do we learn about the Holy Spirit from the Acts of the Apostles?
1. He is the Agent of Conversion –
- the Ethiopian 8:29; Saul 9:17; Cornelius 10:44; Lydia 16:14.
- We are **born** of the Spirit Jn 3:5-8. We are sealed with the promised Holy Spirit – he is the **deposit** guaranteeing our inheritance Eph 1:13
- God saved us through the washing of **rebirth and renewal** by the Holy Spirit whom he **poured out on us generously** Tit 3:5,6.

2. He is the Agent of Christian Maturity -
- The Holy Spirit is active in us. Our body is the temple of the Holy Spirit 1Cor 6:19. The **fruit of the Spirit** appears in our lives as a sign of his work in us Gal 5:22. He is changing us, **transforming us** to be like Christ 2Cor 3:18
- We are **baptized** in the Spirit so we will have **power** to be witnesses to Jesus 1:5,8. He is the source of joy, peace and abounding hope Rom 15:13. We worship in Spirit and in truth Jn 4:24; Rev 1:10; 4:2.
- **Fresh filling** is an ongoing experience 4:8; 7:55; 13:9,52.

3. He is the Agent of Service –
- **Gifts of the Spirit** are given to each one of us – it is the role of leaders to identify and release the gifts - to **equip the saints** for our part in building up the body and in fulfilling God's plan for the world Eph 4:7-16; Rom 12:6; 1Cor 7:7; 12:7,11
- All prayer is through the Holy Spirit who intercedes for us Rom 8:26,27.

4. He is the Agent of Growth – fulfilling the Great Commission
- **in Jerusalem** - Pentecost; Peter's power to witness; the birth of the Church
- **in Judea** – Stephen's power to serve; they were scattered by persecution
- **in Samaria** - Philip found himself in Samaria – then in Gaza
- **to the ends of the earth** – Paul's call to Antioch, Asia, then to Europe.

The Person and Work of the Holy Spirit

The Trinity – The Holy Spirit is the Third PERSON of the Godhead – Father, Son and Holy Spirit 2Cor 13:14.

In the Old Testament the Holy Spirit outworked the purposes of God by anointing individuals with power, for a purpose and a time. He came on them – Gideon Jud 6:34; Samson Jud 13:25; 14:6; Saul 1Sam 10:10; David 1Sam 16:13; Ps 51:11. They spoke by the Spirit Acts 28:25.

The Holy Spirit was active throughout the life of Jesus – in the conception Mt 1:18; in the baptism Mt 3:16; in the Temptation Mt 4:1.

God promised that he would pour out the Holy Spirit on his people in the last days when the Messiah came to enable them to establish his kingdom Is 44:3; Ezk 36:26-28; Joel 2:28 -

- I will pour out my Spirit on all people, your sons and daughters
- before the coming of the great and dreadful day of the Lord
- everyone who calls on the name of the Lord will be saved.

The Seven-fold Ministry of the Holy Spirit

Jesus taught about the purpose of the coming of the Holy Spirit with power which would occur once he had ascended -

- The Father will give you another (same) Counselor – one called in to assist - to be with you forever. He will be in you Jn 14:15-17
- He will teach and remind you of everything Jesus has said Jn 14:26
- He will testify and cause you to testify about Jesus Jn 15:26,27
- He will be with the believer in the same way that he was with his disciples Jn 16:7
- He will convict the heart of guilt, sin, righteousness and judgment Jn 16:8
- He will guide you into all truth and bring glory to Jesus Jn 16:13-15
- He will empower the believer to be an effective witness about Jesus 1:8.

The Holy Spirit in the Life of the Believer
The New Birth

When a person puts their trust in Jesus Christ as Savior and Lord they are born again – born of the Spirit and the Word of God Jn 1:12; 3:3-8; 1Pet 1:23. They receive Eternal Life Acts 13:48.

Repent and be baptized, every one of you in the name of Jesus Christ for the forgiveness of your sins. And you will receive the gift of the Holy

Spirit. The promise is for you and your children and for all who are far off – for all whom the Lord our God will call Acts 2:38,39.
Our body becomes the dwelling place of the Holy Spirit 1Cor 6:19. He begins the sanctifying work of changing us to be like Jesus 2Cor 3:16-18.

The Filling of the Holy Spirit
The outworking of the Holy Spirit requires our submission and obedience Acts 5:32. He will fill us with power to enable us to be witnesses to Jesus. To receive the filling of the Holy Spirit one must –
- believe the promise of Jesus Acts 1:8
- ask believing that you will be filled Lk 11:13
- receive in faith God's gift in faith Acts 1:4-5
- express thanks for having received the in-filling Heb 13:15.

The filling of the Holy Spirit is an ongoing experience as we are responsive to him day by day and are active in his service Eph 5:18-20.

Fruit of the Spirit
The Fruit of the Spirit in our lives is evidence of the sanctifying presence of the Holy Spirit. He works in us, changing our character, our thoughts, actions, motives, speech, our attitude towards sin.

The Fruit is singular and has many facets which equate to the nature and character of God. The fruit is perfectly represented in the life of Jesus Christ. We must expect all of the fruit to be progressively developing in the life of the spirit-filled believer.

The Holy Spirit replaces the worldly character in us and produces the qualities of God. This process is described in Gal 5:16-25 -

1. Love – the self-giving 'agape' love of God 1Cor 13:4-13; Rom 5:5

2. Joy – unspeakable, complete, independent of circumstances and beyond explanation Jn 15:11; 1Pet 1:8

3. Peace – wellbeing, beyond understanding Jn 14:27; Phil 4:7

4. Patience – forbearing, perseverance 2Cor 4:16-19; Jas 1:2-4

5. Kindness – understanding, compassion, caring, helping others

6. Goodness – purity, holiness, godliness - right standing

7. Gentleness – humility, compassion, thankfulness, no self-praise

8. Faithfulness – believing and acting, persistence, maturity, never giving up

9. Self control – discipline, obedience, submission to the Holy Spirit.

Other Fruit of the Spirit

- **Beatitudes** – poor in spirit, mournful, meek, hungry and thirsty for righteousness, pure in heart, peacemaker, persecuted for Jesus Mt 5:1-16
- **Faith, Hope, Love** 1Cor 13:13; Rom 15:13 - always abounding
- **Considerate, submissive, merciful, impartial, sincere** Jas 3:17
- **Unity** - the Spirit brings unity – make every effort to keep it! Eph 4:3
- **Forgiveness** – of others in the same way we are forgiven Mt 18:21-35
- **Repentance** – recognition of sin and immediate response to turn away
- **Honesty** – truthful in word and deed
- **Integrity** - genuine in all situations.
- **Contentment** – Thankfull in all circumstances Phil 4:11-13

Jesus said **'By their fruit you will recognize them'** Mt 7:15-20.

Gifts of the Holy Spirit

Each member is given a gift from God. The gifts are given for the common good – for the building up of the Body of Christ 1Cor 12:7,11. We each have different gifts Rom 12:6 - we expect gifts in each believer. The gifts belong to the Holy Spirit who gives them just as he determines 1Cor 12:11. That is why we must humbly keep seeking his leading! It is not that a person uses the gifts of the Holy Spirit – the Holy Spirit who fills the person **uses that person** according to his own will, time and situation to edify the Church as the person is responsive. The gifts are for giving. God has made us dependent on one another – we are each members of the Body of Christ 1Cor 12:27. The Body builds itself up as each member works effectively using the gifts the Spirit produces in them Eph 4:7-16. The outcome of the use of the gifts is that God will receive glory. We must fan into flame the gift of God 2Tim 1:6. Eagerly desire the greater spiritual gifts - that serve others 1Cor 12:31. We are working together with God! 2Cor 5:14, 20; 6:1.

Spiritual Gifts - 1 Corinthians 12:7-11

1. Message of Wisdom - to know through revelation specific understanding in regard to a subject or a given situation Jn 8:7 (1)

2. Message of Knowledge - to know the mind of the Holy Spirit for a specific need in the daily life and ministry of the Body of Christ Acts 5:34 (2)

3. Faith – to believe and accomplish acts for God. Faith must be based on God and the promises of his Word Mt 17:20 (3)

4. Healing – to act as an intermediary or channel through whom God cures illness and restores health and wholeness Mt 8:16,17; 1Pet 2:24 (4)

5. Miracles – to act as an intermediary or channel through whom God performs a powerful deed outside of the course of nature (5) Acts 3:1-6

6. Prophecy – to speak forth a message or word from God to instruct, edify, exhort, encourage or comfort the Body of believers (6)

7. Distinguishing between spirits – to know with assurance if behavior is from human or evil origin Mt 16:16,17,23 (7)

8. Tongues – to speak in an unlearned language which edifies the speaker or communicates a message to the Body. The gift of tongues deepens the spiritual life of the believer and needs interpretation 1Cor 14:4 (8)

9. Interpretation of Tongues – to make known through inspiration the message spoken in tongues 1Cor 14:13 (9)

Ministry Gifts - Ephesians 4:11

1. Apostle – to be sent out with authority - to establish a work (10)

2. Prophet – to operate the gift of prophecy regularly over a period (6)

3. Evangelist – to minister specifically in sharing the Gospel (11)

4. Pastor – to exercise personal ministry and responsibility for the spiritual welfare of a group of believers for a period (12)

5. Teacher – to communicate information relevant to the spiritual welfare of the body of believers Acts 11:22-26 (13)

Service Gifts - Romans 12:6-8

1. Prophecy – (6)

2. Serving – to identify and contribute to needs of others Mt 20:25-28 (14)

3. Teaching – (13)

4. Encouraging – to minister words and acts of comfort, counsel and encouragement for the wellbeing of others (15)

5. Contributing – giving of one's abilities, material resources and time to the work of the Lord Acts 11:27-30 (16)

6. Leadership – to motivate and assist others to achieve an agreed goal (17)

7. Mercy – to feel and share empathy with another Jn 8:1-11 (18)

Other Gifts of the Spirit

1. Helps – to invest ability in the work of ministry 1Cor 12:28 (19)

2. Administration – to organize people and resources to achieve the goals of the Body 1Cor 12:28 (20)

3. Celibacy – to remain single in order to devote time to the work of the ministry 1Cor 7:7,8 (21)

4. Poverty – to forgo wellbeing to minister to others 1Cor 13:3 (22)

5. Martyrdom – to undergo suffering for the faith 1Cor 13:3 (23)

6. Hospitality – to provide service for others Rom 12:9-13 (24)

7. Mission – to minister to another culture 1Cor 9:19-23 (25)

8. Intercession – to pray regularly for specific needs Jas 5:15-18 (26)

9. Exorcism – to cast out demons or evil spirits Acts 13:6-12 (27)

10. Practical skills – abilities and knowledge in all kinds of craft – to be used for God's glory Ex 31:3 (28)

All abilities – intellect, talents and skills are gifts from God to be yielded to the Holy Spirit Mt 25:14-30.
He will multiply them and use them in the most effective way for the kingdom Jn 6:5-14.

References

1. Dr Paul Yonggi Cho, *The Holy Spirit, My Senior Partner,* Word, UK, 1989. p13.
2. Dr F F Bruce, *The New Testament Documents,* Inter-Varsity Press, London, 1972, pp 15,113.
3. Josh McDowell, *Evidence That Demands a Verdict,* Campus Crusade for Christ, California, 1977, p 83.
4. Dr Chuck Missler, *Cosmic Codes,* Koinonia House, California, 2004, p409.
5. Charles Finney, *Power from on High,* Whitaker House, Pennsylvania, 1996, p20.
6. LeRoy Eims, *The Lost Art of Disciple Making,* Zondadervan, Michagan, 1978, pp22,59.
7. Dr Paul Yonggi Cho, *Successful Home Cell Groups,* Lockman Foundation, California, 1977, p58.
8. Thomas Phillips, *The Welsh Revival,* Banner of Truth, Edinburgh, 1995, p122.
9. Stephen Hawking, *A Brief History of Time*, Bantam, New York, 1988, p131
10. Fred Hoyle, *The Universe: Some Past and Present Reflections,* Engineering and Science, 1981.
11. Bertrand Russel, *Essays on Religion,* Simon and Schuster, New York, 1957.
12. M Staniforth, *Early Christian Writings,* Penguin Books, Middlesex, 1968, p8,89.
13. T C Hammond, *In Understanding Be Men,* Billings, London, 1963, p 20.
14. J Stevenson, *A New Eusebius, Documents illustrative of the history of the Church to AD 337,* S.P.C.K., London, 1970, p155.
15. G A Williamson, *The History of the Church,* Penguin Books, Middlesex, 1965.

BOOKS OF THE BIBLE
[39 + 27 = 66]

BOOKS OF THE OLD TESTAMENT
[39]

	HISTORY (17)	POETRY (5)	PROPHECY (17)	
LAW (5)	Genesis	Job	Isaiah	**MAJOR (5)**
Pentateuch	Exodus	Psalms	Jeremiah	
Books of Moses	Leviticus	Proverbs	Lamentations	
	Numbers	Ecclesiastes	Ezekiel	
	Deuteronomy	Solomon	Daniel	
HISTORY (12)	Joshua		Hosea	**MINOR (12)**
of Israel	Judges		Joel	
	Ruth		Amos	
	1 Samuel		Obadiah	
	2 Samuel		Jonah	
	1 Kings		Micah	
	2 Kings		Nahum	
	1 Chronicles		Habakkuk	
	2 Chronicles		Zephaniah	
	Ezra	Post Exile	Haggai	
	Nehemiah		Zechariah	
	Esther		Malachi	

BOOKS OF THE NEW TESTAMENT
[27]

	HISTORY (5)	LETTERS OF PAUL (13)	GENERAL LETTERS (9)	
GOSPELS (4)	Matthew	Romans	Hebrews	Unknown
	Mark	1 Corinthians	James	Other
	Luke	2 Corinthians	1 Peter	Apostles (7)
	John	Glatians	2 Peter	
Early Church (1)	Acts	Ephesians	1 John	
Luke		Philippians	2 John	
		Colossians	3 John	
		1 Thessalonians	Jude	
		2 Thessalonians	Revelation	John
		1 Timothy		
		2 Timothy		
		Titus		
		Philemon		

The Layman's Commentary Series contains the following -